THE POSTER

1,000 POSTERS FROM TOULOUSE-LAUTREC TO SAGMEISTER

Edited by
Cees W. de Jong

Alston W. Purvis
Martijn F. Le Coultre

Text by
Alston W. Purvis

Introduction by
Cees W. de Jong

THE POSTER

ABRAMS, NEW YORK

CONTENTS

Cees W. de Jong

Alston W. Purvis

THE TIMES

For 7th NOVEMBER, 1805

BATTLE OF
TRAFALGAR

CAPTURE OF
FRENCH & SPANISH FLEETS

DEATH OF NELSON

List of Killed and Wounded

6

No. 0001
Artist unknown
Battle of Trafalgar, 1805
The Times, London
51 x 38 cm

INTRODUCTION: DELIVER THE MESSAGE

For more than ten thousand years we have felt the need to express ourselves with writing and drawing. Since the Neolithic period, we have communicated not only through gestures and sound but also by means of a visual language. Worldwide, hunters and gatherers and later early farmers made use of information systems to advertise services and products. It was also a way of maintaining facts and data. From the beginning visual language was highly important and is still relevant today.

Looking back on the last hundred and thirty years of poster design, the initial development of the poster usually included typography and the use of some type of illustration, and the purpose of the poster has always been to deliver a message. A simple, practical medium requiring paper, ink, and an idea, the poster has remained essentially unchanged from the industrial revolution until today.

All people are limited in their ability to process information and acclimate to innovation, and the speed of change has increased exponentially in the globalized world that we live in today. Making efficient use of the new media available helps to develop and stimulate the creative process, and with the new technology designers' roles have changed. Project execution has become one of multiple roles; the designer must be able to simultaneously serve as content manager, designer, typographer, illustrator, and photographer. There are increasing demands for the designer to be involved in all aspects of the work.

The digital era has transformed the world of communication, design, and typography, with breathtaking advances in recent decades. Technology's impact on poster design and the ways in which contemporary designers are harnessing the visual language of the past to satisfy the needs of the present and future are evident in this selection of 1,000 posters.

I would like to express my appreciation to all of the poster designers and collectors for their support in the writing of this book. Special thanks are extended to Martijn F. Le Coultre, collector; Jelle van der Toorn Vrijthoff, designer and International President of AGI; and Udo Boersma, of Van Sabben Poster Auctions, for their advice. It was a pleasure to work together again on this book with Alston W. Purvis, Chair of the Graphic Design Department at the Boston University College of Fine Arts.

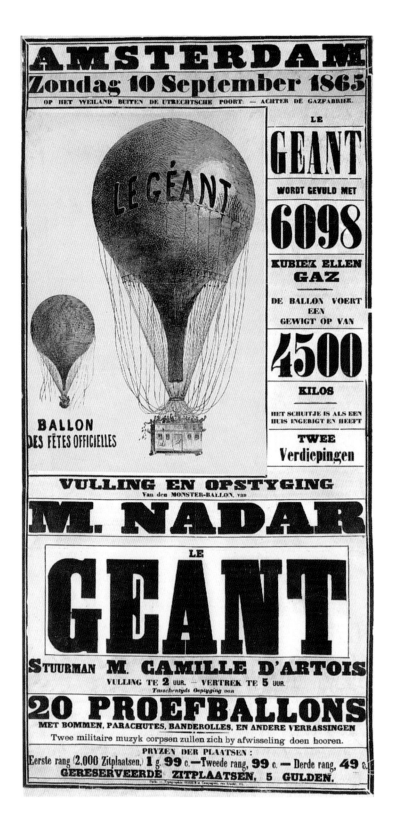

No. 0002
Artist unknown
M. Nadar, Le Géant, 1865
Imp. Lemercier, Paris
With pasted-on engraving,
183 x 87 cm

No. 0003
Frans Van Kuyck
(1852-1915)
*International Exhibition of
Antwerp*, 1885
Imp. Typo-Lithographie
Ratinckx Frères, Antwerp
255 x 120 cm

No. 0004
Henri de Toulouse-Lautrec
(1864-1901)
*Reine de joie par Victor
Joze* (poster to publicize a
novel), 1892
Edw. Ancourt, Paris
146 x 96 cm

THE MAGNETISM OF POSTERS

The *Oxford English Dictionary* concisely defines a poster as "a placard posted or displayed in a public place as an announcement or advertisement." However, in 1901, the art historian Raymond Needham provided far more specific guidelines for what a successful poster should entail: "Take any representative Japanese print—a book illustration, a broad sheet or a theater bill—and it will be found to embody all that a good poster should. One dominant idea is presented graphically, beautifully. The detail does not weaken, but actually enforces the motif. There is not a superfluous line. The color scheme of flat tints is fresh and striking, but always harmonious. The composition gives an idea of balance and breadth, but affords no hint as to how these qualities have been attained. . . . The general effect is decorative in the highest degree, may be humorous and is certainly pervaded by the 'hidden soul of harmony.'"

A poster consists of two means of communication, words and images, and these are often used together. A successful poster should instantly grasp the attention of the onlooker and maintain it until the communication has been conveyed. The main objective of a poster is to deliver a message or endorse a product, cause, or event. A poster's effectiveness is determined by a number of qualities, including distinctiveness, lucidity, and, without exception, a striking design. This last facet was especially important during the latter half of the nineteenth century when posters were often displayed together with other designs in "hoardings." Thus, to be noticed, a poster had to be conspicuous among its competitors.

No. 0005

Henri de Toulouse-Lautrec
(1864-1901)
Ambassadeurs (poster for a
cabaret act), 1892
Edw. Ancourt, Paris
140 x 95 cm

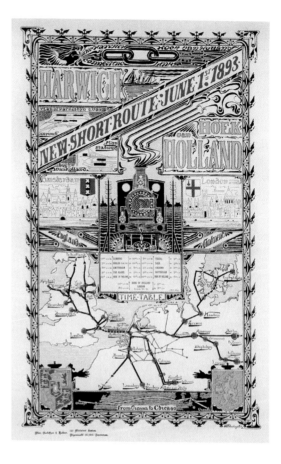

No. 0006

Carloz Schwabe

(1866-1926)

Salon Rose Croix

(exhibition poster), 1892

Draeger & Lesieur, imp.

Verdoux, Ducourtioux &

Huillard, Paris

197 x 84 cm

No. 0007

Hendrik Petrus Berlage

(1856-1934)

Harwich-Hoek Van Holland,

1893

Phot. Roelofzen & Hübner,

Amsterdam

98 x 60 cm

No. 0008

Pierre Bonnard

(1867-1947)

La Revue Blanche (poster

promoting a periodical),

1894

Edw. Ancourt, Paris

87.5 x 69 cm

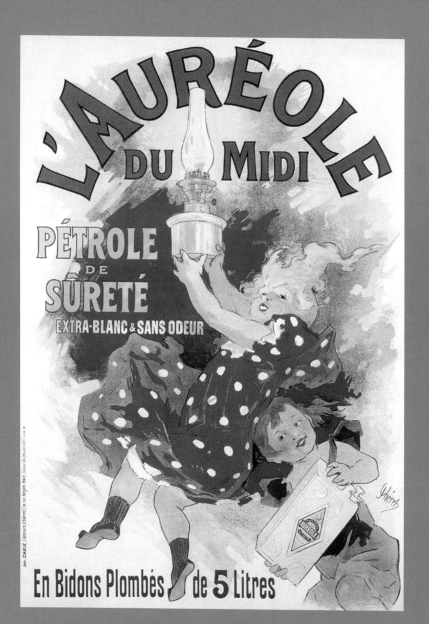

14

No. 0009
Jules Chéret (1836-1932)
L'Auréole du Midi (poster
advertising lamp oil), 1893
Imp. Chaix (Ateliers
Chéret), Paris
121 x 84 cm

TURN OF THE 19TH CENTURY AND ART NOUVEAU

At first, posters were dismissed as ephemera and were usually thrown away shortly after achieving their intended objectives. Those that were fortunately saved offer valuable insight into the societies they represent, and many are now regarded as icons of their respective cultures. Finally, by the 1890s, especially in France and England, posters began to be valued as collectable works of art.

Initially called *style moderne*, Art Nouveau was named after the Salon de l'Art Nouveau in Paris started by Samuel Bing in 1895. Art Nouveau would eventually encompass all of the arts, including architecture, painting, the arts and crafts, vases, furniture, ornament, books, and especially posters. Never in any sense a unified movement, it had various labels: Art Nouveau in France and Belgium; Nieuwe Kunst in the Netherlands; and Jugendstil in Germany, Austria, and other European countries. Inspiration came from such diverse sources as organic plant forms, stained glass, Celtic manuscripts, the Dutch East Indies, Japanese *ukiyo-e* woodblock prints, and decorative forms from India, Syria, Egypt, and Persia. Although Art Nouveau posters exhibited national traits, they shared many common characteristics, among them a fascination with winding and undulating lines, flat areas of color, organic patterns, an elegant harmony, and a complex and esoteric symbolism.

Nikolaus Pevsner's 1936 book *Pioneers of Modern Design* was one of the first publications to allot Art Nouveau an important role in twentieth-century modern art and architecture. He described the movement's main attributes as "the long sensitive curve, reminiscent of the lily's stem, an insect's feeler, the filament of a blossom or occasionally a slender flame, the curve undulating, flowing and interplaying with others, sprouting from corners and covering asymmetrically all available surfaces."

The appellation "father of the modern poster" is often bestowed upon the French artist Jules Chéret. A skillful technician in addition to his artistic talents, Chéret attained a dazzling range of colors using red, yellow, and blue as a basic palette. A characteristic Chéret poster often displays a large, graceful, and animated female figure with the stylized hair frequently associated with Art Nouveau. The iconic free-spirited models in his posters were affectionately referred to as "Chér-ettes," and inspired many French women to assume more liberated roles in society.

The boisterous nightlife of la belle époque in Paris inspired poster artists and brought them commissions. Among the artists often seen at Le Chat Noir were Henri de Toulouse-Lautrec and the Swiss Théophile-Alexandre Steinlen, who created posters for the nightclub. Toulouse-Lautrec avidly frequented Paris cabarets and bordellos, observing and participating. Although he produced only thirty-one posters, Toulouse-Lautrec profoundly affected the course of French poster design.

The Czech artist Alphonse Mucha arrived in Paris at the age of twenty-seven, and his work soon began to rival that of Chéret. His recurring subject matter consisted of elegant female figures amid stylized forms taken from sources such as plants and Byzantine art. By 1900 his posters were so popular that *l'art nouveau* was often referred to as *le style Mucha*.

15

16

No. 0010

Dudley Hardy(1867-1922)

A Gaiety Girl, 1894

Waterlow & Sons, London

226 x 98.5 cm

No. 0011

Aubrey Vincent Beardsley

(1872-1898)

Children's Books, 1894

T. Fisher Unwin, London

75.5 x 51 cm

No. 0012

Théophile-Alexandre

Steinlen (1859-1923)

Lait Pur Stérilisé (poster for

sterilized milk), 1894

Imp. Charles Verneau, Paris

135 x 99 cm

No. 0013
Manuel Orazi (1860-1934)
Thaïs (opera poster), 1894
Imp. Lemercier, Paris
101 x 64 cm

No. 0014
Henri Cassiers (1858-1944)
Red Star Line, Anvers New York, 1898
Lith. O. De Rycker &
Mendel, Brussels
Metal strip, 47 x 83 cm

No. 0015
Jan Theodoor Toorop
(1858-1928)
Delftsche Slaolie (poster for a salad-oil company), 1894
S. Lankhout & Co., The Hague, The Netherlands
100 x 70 cm

20

No. 0016
Arthur Sjögren (1874-1951)
Stora Bryggeriets Öl (beer
poster), 1895
Künstnerliga Affischer,
Stockholm
84.5 x 57.5 cm

No. 0017
Beggarstaff Brothers
(James Pryde, 1869-1941,
and William Nicholson,
1872-1949)
"Kassama" Corn Flower,
1894
Henderson & Co., Glasgow
147 x 98 cm

No. 0018
Caran d'Ache (1859-1909)
Exposition Russe, 1895
Imp. Hérold, Paris
135.5 x 87.5 cm

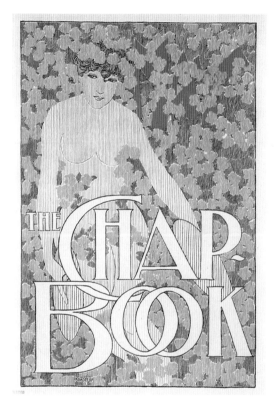

No. 0019
William H. Bradley
(1868-1962)
The Chap Book, 1895
USA
52.5 x 35.5 cm

No. 0020
Beggarstaff Brothers
(James Pryde, 1869-1941,
and William Nicholson,
1872-1949)
Collage for a poster, c. 1895
UK
225 x 139.3 cm

No. 0021
Jules Chéret (1836-1932)
Pastilles Géraudel (poster
advertising cough drops),
1895
Imp. Chaix (Ateliers
Chéret), Paris
121.5 x 87 cm

23

24

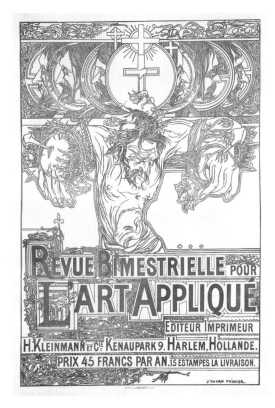

No. 0022

Artist unknown (circle of
William H. Bradley)
The Stafford Fountain Pen,
c. 1896
Forbes, Boston
98 x 69 cm

No. 0023

Wilhelm Christiaan Georg
Rueter (1875-1966)
De Hinde (poster for a
bicycle company), 1896
Lith. Gebr. Braakensiek,
Amsterdam
106 x 82 cm

No. 0024

Johan Thorn Prikker
(1888-1932)
*Revue Bimestrielle pour
l'Art Appliqué*, 1896
Lith. S. Lankhout, The
Hague, The Netherlands
135 x 100.5 cm

No. 0025

Edward Penfield (1866-
1925)
Harper's October, 1896
Harper & Brothers, New
York
35 x 46 cm

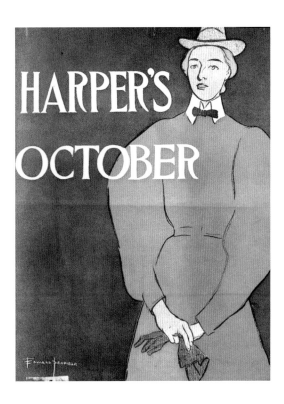

27

No. 0026
Théophile-Alexandre
Steinlen (1859-1923)
Affiches Charles Verneau
(poster for a poster
publisher), 1896
Imp. Charles Verneau, Paris
235 x 304 cm

28

No. 0027

Théophile-Alexandre
Steinlen (1859-1923)
Tournée du Chat Noir
(cabaret poster,) 1896
Imp. Charles Verneau, Paris
140.5 x 100 cm

No. 0028

Alphonse Mucha
(1860-1939)
Champagne Ruinart, 1896
Lith. F. Champenois, Paris
175 x 60 cm

No. 0029

Alphonse Mucha
(1860-1939)
La Dame aux Camelias
(theater poster), 1896
Lith. F. Champenois, Paris
205 x 71 cm

No. 0030
Jules Chéret (1836-1932)
Taverne Olympia, 1899
Courrier Français
supplement, Imp. Chaix
(Ateliers Chéret), Paris
39.5 x 57 cm

No. 0031
Jules Chéret (1836-1932)
Bal Masque (poster for a
masquerade ball), 1891
Imp. Courrier *Français*
supplement, Imp. Chaix
(Ateliers Chéret), Paris
39.5 x 57 cm

No. 0032
Alphonse Mucha
(1860-1939)
*Moët & Chandon, Grand
Crémant Imperial*, 1899
Imp. F. Champenois, Paris
On linen, 24.5 x 62.5 cm

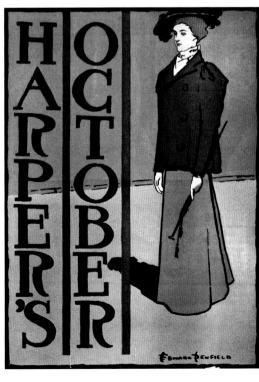

No. 0033
Ethel Reed (b. 1876)
In Childhood's Country,
1895
Geo H. Walker & Co, Boston
29.5 x 63.5 cm

No. 0034
Ethel Reed (b. 1876)
Arabella and Araminta, 1895
Geo H. Walker & Co, Boston
39.5 x 68.5 cm

No. 0035
Edward Penfield (1866-1925)
Harper's October, 1897
Harper & Brothers,
New York
36 x 49.5 cm

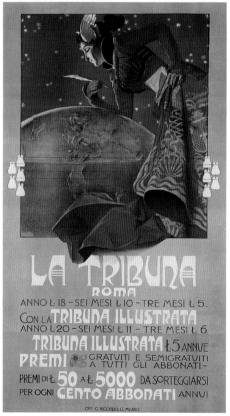

No. 0036
Viktor Oliva (1861-1928)
Topicuv Salon (exhibition
poster), 1896
Imp. Chaix, Paris
41 x 28 cm

No. 0037
Giovanni S. A. Mataloni
(1869-1944)
La Tribuna Roma
(newspaper poster), 1897
Officine G. Ricordi & C.,
Milan
245 x 138 cm

No. 0038
George Frederick Scotson-
Clark (b. 1873)
*Mathews & Bulger at Gay
Coney Island*, 1897
The Enquirer Job Printing
Co., Cincinnati
108.5 x 74.5 cm

No. 0039
Edmund Edel (1863-1934)
Simplicissimus (poster for a
satirical magazine), 1900
Hollerbaum & Schmidt,
Berlin
137.5 x 93.5 cm

33

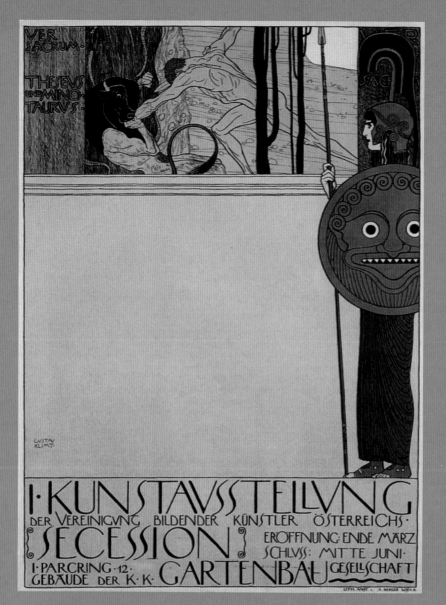

No. 0040
Gustav Klimt (1862-1918)
*1. Kunstausstellung
Secession* (exhibition
poster), 1898
Lith. Anst. v. A. Berger,
Vienna
63.5 x 46 cm

THE VIENNA SECESSION

The Vienna Secession (the Sezessionstil) began on April 3, 1897, when the younger and more activist associates of the Künstlerhaus, the Vienna creative artists group, walked out in protest over what they considered the organization's excessively conservative stances. Secessionists included the architects Joseph Maria Olbrich and Josef Hoffmann and the painters Koloman Moser and Gustav Klimt. Klimt's poster design of 1898 for the first Secessionist exhibition shows Athena observing the battle between Theseus and the Minotaur. The use of open space was highly unusual for poster design at the time. Olbrich's poster for the 1898 Secession exhibition demonstrates a clear affinity with the Glasgow School. After 1910 the creative thrust of the Sezessionstil began to weaken. However, their workshops endured the turmoil of World War I and continued until 1932, when economic problems caused their closure.

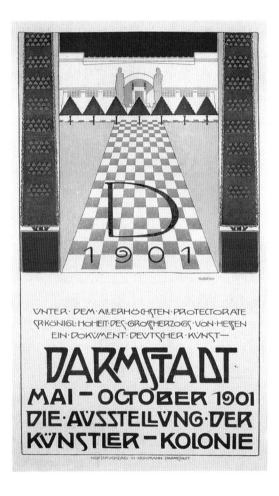

No. 0041

Joseph Maria Olbrich
(1867-1908)
Darmstadt (exhibition
poster), 1901
Hofdruckerei H. Hofman,
Darmstadt, Germany
86 x 50 cm

No. 0042

Joseph Maria Olbrich
(1867-1908)
Secession (exhibition
poster), 1898
Lith. Anst. v. A. Berger,
Vienna
86.5 x 46 cm

No. 0043

Georges de Feure
(1868-1928)
Le Journal des Ventes, 1899
Imp. Lemercier, Paris
61 x 41 cm

No. 0044

Henri Privat-Livemont
(1861-1936)
J. C. Boldoot, 1899
Van Leer, Amsterdam
75 x 40 cm

No. 0045

Johann Georg van Caspel
(1870-1924)
W. Hoogenstraaten (poster
advertising vegetable
soups and sauces), 1899
Lith. Senefelder, Amsterdam
74 x 52 cm

No. 0046

Adolf Boehm (1861-1927)
VIII. Ausstellung Secession
(exhibition poster), 1900
Lith. u. Druck A. Berger,
Vienna
95 x 64cm

No. 0047

Franz Laskoff (1869-1918)
E&A Mele & Ci (poster for a
department store), 1900
Officine G. Ricordi & C.,
Milan
200 x 142 cm

No. 0048

Heinrich Leffler
(1863-1919)
Kunst und Kunsthandwerk
(exhibition poster), c. 1899
Verlag von Artaria, Vienna
63.5 x 45.5 cm

No. 0049

Edmund Edel (1863-1934)
Berliner Secessions Bühne
(exhibition poster), 1900
Hollerbaum & Schmidt,
Berlin
137.5 x 93.5 cm

40

d Star Line
lew York

No. 0050
Henri Cassiers (1858-1944)
Red Star Line, 1899
Lith. O. de Rycker &
Mendel, Brussels
113.5 x 154.5 cm

No. 0051

Manuel Orazi (1860-1934)
Théatre de Loie Fuller, 1900
Affiches Artistiques Manuel
Orazi, Paris
198.5 x 61.5 cm

No. 0052

Alphonse Mucha
(1860-1939)
Salon des Cent (exhibition
poster), 1896
Imp. F. Champenois, Paris
43 x 63 cm

43

No. 0053
Maurice Biais (1860-1934)
La Maison Moderne (poster
for a home decor store),
c. 1898
Imp. Artistique J. Minot,
Paris
115 x 79.5 cm

No. 0054
Franz Laskoff (1869-1918)
Caffaro (poster advertising
a newspaper), c. 1901
Officine G. Ricordi & C., Milan
202 x 144 cm

No. 0055
Johann Victor Krämer
(1861-1949)
XI. Ausstellung Secession
(exhibition poster), 1901
Albert Berger, Vienna
123.5 x 90 cm

BENZO-MOTEUR
Essence spéciale
POUR AUTOMOBILES
en Bidons Plombés & Capsulés

No. 0056

Jules Chéret (1836-1932)
Benzo-Moteur (motor oil),
1900
Imp. Chaix (Ateliers
Chéret), Paris
117 x 87 cm

No. 0057

Jacques Villon (1875-1963)
Guinguette Fleurie (cabaret
poster), 1901
E. Malfeyt, Paris
129 x 93 cm

No. 0058

Ludwig Hohlwein (1874-
1949)
Ernemann Prismengläser,
c. 1913
Fritz Maison, Munich
35 x 50 cm

No. 0059
Vladimir Zupansky
(1869-1928)
*Collectiv Ausstellung
des Bildhauers A. Rodin*
(exhibition poster), 1902
Unie, Prague
158 x 80 cm

No. 0060
Marcello Dudovich
(1878-1962)
Bitter Campari, 1901
E. Chappuis, Bologna
137 x 96 cm

No. 0061
Leonetto Cappiello
(1875-1942)
Absinthe Ducros Fils, 1901
Imp. P. Vercasson, Paris
134.5 x 96.5 cm

No. 0062

N. N. Gerardov (1873-
1919)
The Fairy-Tale Ball, 1901
R. Golike, St. Petersburg
101.5 x 38 cm

No. 0063

Heinrich Leffler
(1863-1919)
Wiener Künstlerbund Hagen
(exhibition poster), 1903
Theodor Eismann, Leipzig
87.5 x 58 cm

No. 0064

Tadeusz Brzozowski (1918-
1987)
Wystawa i Jarmark (trade-
fair poster), 1905
Karola Kranikowsiego,
Poland
100 x 69.5 cm

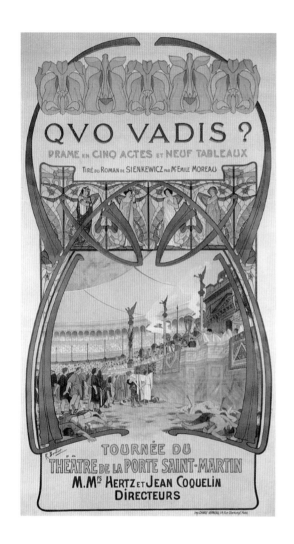

50

No. 0065
Robert Boullier
Quo Vadis (theater poster),
c. 1905
Imp. Charles Verneau, Paris
193 x 104 cm

No. 0066
Artist unknown
Horch (poster for an
automobile company),
c. 1905
Moritz Prescher Nchfgr.
A. G. Leutsch/Leipzig,
Germany
120.5 x 89.5 cm

No. 0067
Leonetto Cappiello
(1875-1942)
Chocolat Klaus, 1903
P. Vercasson & Cie., Paris
157 x 114 cm

CHOCOLAT
KLAUS

Imp. P. VERCASSON & Cie 43, rue de Lancry, PARIS.

52

LITH. S. LANKHOUT & C? HAAC

No. 0068
Johan Thorn Prikker
(1888-1932)
Holländische Kunst-
ausstellung in Krefeld
(exhibition poster), 1903
Lith. S. Lankhout & Co.,
The Hague, The Netherlands.
85 x 119 cm

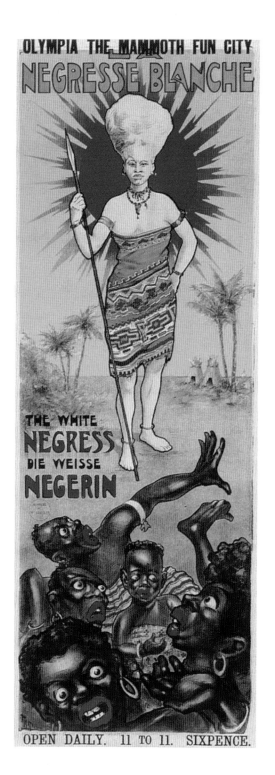

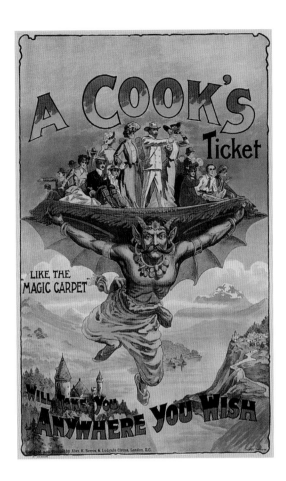

No. 0069

Candido Aragonese de
Faria (1849-1911)
La Negresse Blanche,
c. 1905
Affiches Faria, Paris
159 x 57 cm

No. 0070

Artist unknown
*Col. W. F. Cody "Buffalo
Bill"* (poster for the Wild
West show), 1908
The Strobridge Litho Co.,
Cincinnati & New York,
three sheets, on linen
98 x 207 cm

No. 0071

Alex K. Sutton
A Cook's Ticket (poster for
travel agent), 1907
London
100 x 62 cm

No. 0072

Daniël (Daan) Hoeksema
(1879-1935)
Simplex (bicycle poster),
1907
Lith. Senefelder, Amsterdam
114.5 x 52.5 cm

56

No. 0073

Adolf Karpellus
(1869-1919)
Künstlerhaus XXXIII Jahres-Ausstellung (exhibition
poster), 1907
K. u. K. Hofl. J. Weiner,
Vienna
122 x 93 cm

No. 0074

Hans Rudi Erdt (1883-1918)
Bar Riche, 1907
Vereinigte Druckereien
& Kunstanstalten vorm.
Schön & Maison G.m.b.H.,
Munich
125 x 89.5 cm

No. 0075

Ludwig Hohlwein
(1874-1949)
Confection Kehl (poster for
a menswear store), 1908
Graph. Anstalt J. E.
Wolfensberger, Zürich
122 x 92 cm

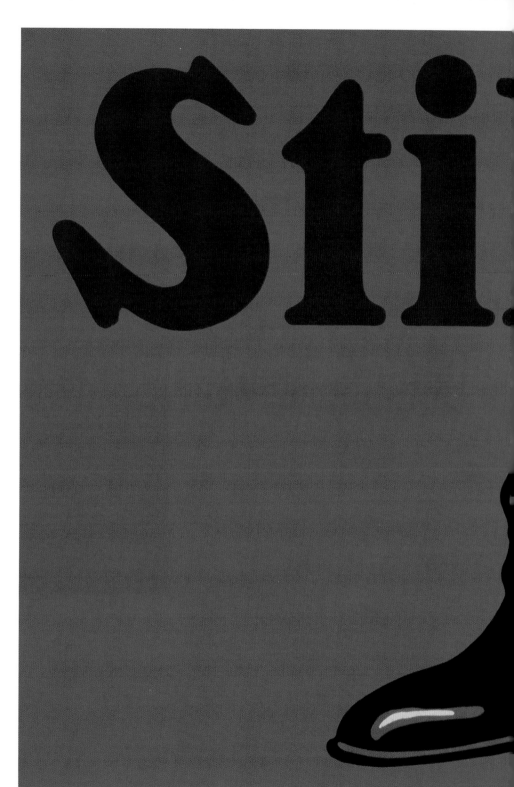

No. 0076
Lucian Bernhard
(1883-1972)
Stiller (poster for a shoe
company), 1908
Friedewald & Frick, Berlin
70 x 95 cm

60

No. 0077
Ludwig Hohlwein
(1874-1949)
Wilhelm Mozer (restaurant
poster), 1909
G. Schuh & Cie., Munich
121 x 88.5 cm

No. 0078
Heinrich Moser (b. 1886)
Mercedes Berliet, c. 1908
Meisenbach Riffarth,
Munich
115 x 77.5 cm

No. 0079
Emile Cardinaux
(1877-1936)
Zermatt, 1908
Switzerland
103 x 72 cm

61

ZERMATT

MATTERHORN 4505m SCHWEIZ

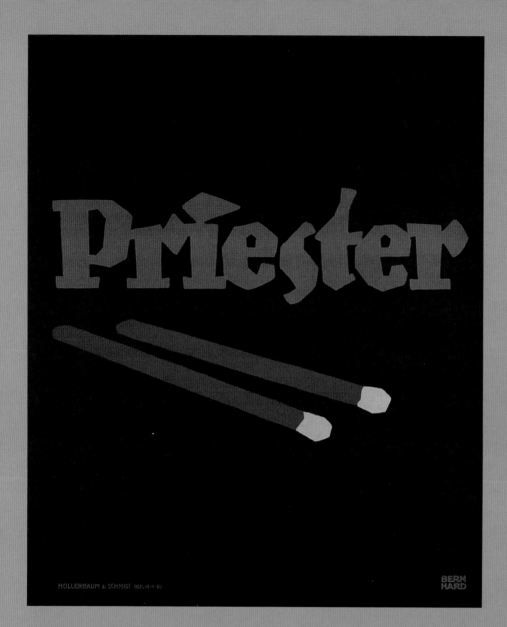

PLAKATSTIL AND WAR

No. 0080
Lucian Bernhard
(1883-1972)
Priester (match company),
1906
Hollerbaum & Schmidt,
Berlin
59.5 x 48.5 cm

Known as the Beggarstaffs, the two British artists and brothers-in-law William Nicholson and James Pryde became friends while in art school and attained respectable reputations as painters before beginning their brief careers as graphic designers in 1894. By using cut paper and lithography, they reduced their images to elementary outlines and flat color areas. The partnership lasted from 1894 to 1899, and produced illustrations, signs, and mainly posters. Unfortunately, they were able to find only a few clients, and no more than a dozen of their poster designs were in fact printed. In spite of this, the posters of the Beggarstaffs would soon be a source of inspiration for many designers in Europe and the United States.

Lucian Bernhard's 1906 design for Priester matches initiated a fundamental transformation in the European approach to advertising posters. The winning entry in a Priester design competition, it showed only two matchsticks and the name Priester on a plain background. Bernhard began with a far more complicated design, replete with dancing girls, a burning cigar, an ashtray, and a tablecloth. The poster was then progressively reduced to the final version. Only eighteen years old and with no art background, Bernhard inspired an entire generation of poster artists. With an emphasis on lucidity and legibility, this style would become known as the "Plakatstil" (which simply means "poster style" in German).

The Berlin printer Hollerbaum & Schmidt understood the significance of the new Plakatstil and gave commissions to some of the designers using this approach. In addition to Bernhard, these included Hans Rudi Erdt and the Austrian-born Julius Klinger.

Undoubtedly, the leading Plakatstil poster artist was the Munich designer Ludwig Hohlwein. Although he was beholden to Bernhard and the Beggarstaffs, the decorative patterns and nuances of color and shade in his elegant posters place them in their own special realm, and his urbane style would have a major impact on European poster design.

Widely utilized by both the Allies and Central Powers, posters were vital propaganda tools during World War I. As part of the war effort, they were used for fund-raising, recruitment, increasing industrial production, the conservation of resources, and volunteer initiatives. It was the largest marketing operation in history: In the United States alone more than 2,500 designs and 20 million posters were printed. Some were blatantly sentimental, such as the British poster "Daddy, what did YOU do during the Great War?" designed by Saville Lumley. Others were more direct, such as James Montgomery Flagg's 1917 poster of Uncle Sam pointing an admonishing finger at a potential recruit. German designers such as Bernhard, Klinger, Gipkins, Erdt, and Hohlwein all rose to the occasion and created immensely effective posters. Their designs contrasted sharply with the more traditional illustrative approach seen in posters for the Allies, and reflected the innovations of the Vienna Secession and the Plakatstil.

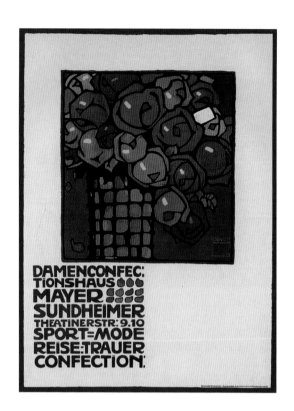

64

No. 0081

Richard Nicolaüs Roland
Holst (1868-1938)
Marsyas (theater poster),
1910
Tresling & Co., Amsterdam
95 x 70.5 cm

No. 0082

Ludwig Hohlwein
(1874-1949)
Mayer Sundheimer (poster
for a boutique), 1909
G. Schuh & Cie., Munich
121 x 88.5 cm

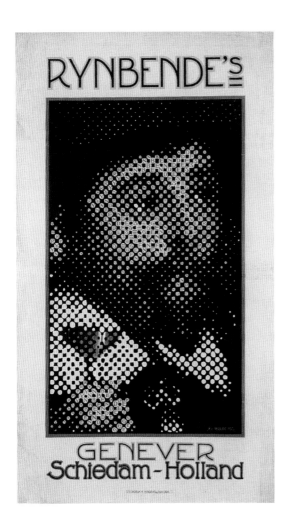

No. 0083

F. van Wolde (1891-1945)
Rynbende's Genever,
c. 1910
Steendruk N. Hindriks
& Zoon, Groningen,
The Netherlands
71.5 x 40.5 cm

No. 0084

Adrien Barrère (1877-1931)
Grand Guignol de Paris,
c. 1910
R. Philippe de Girard, Paris
On linen, 114 x 110.5 cm

No. 0085

Jan Rotgans (1881-1969)
Spyker Auto's, c. 1910
Lith. Lankhout, The Hague,
The Netherlands
147 x 101 cm

No. 0086

Marcello Dudovich
(1878-1962)
Marca Zenit (poster
advertising Borsalino hats),
1911
Officine G. Ricordi & C.,
Milan
203 x 142.5 cm

No. 0087

Artist unknown
L'Amant Fidele, c. 1910
Imp. des Etablissements
Gaumont, Paris
104 x 75.5 cm

No. 0088

Ludwig Hohlwein
(1874-1949)
Starnberger-See, 1910
Reichhold & Lang, Lith.
Kunstanstalt, Munich
93.5 x 125 cm

No. 0089

Ludwig Hohlwein
(1874-1949)
Yellowstone-Park, 1910
G. Schuh & Cie., Munich
124.5 x 91.5 cm

68

No. 0090
Lucian Bernhard
(1883-1972)
Manoli (cigarette poster),
1911
Hollerbaum & Schmidt,
Berlin
69.5 x 96 cm

No. 0091
Lucian Bernhard
(1883-1972)
Manoli (cigarette poster),
1910
Hollerbaum & Schmidt,
Berlin
69.5 x 96 cm

No. 0092
Hans Rudi Erdt
(1883-1918)
Neverfail (poster for a
window manufacturer),
1911
Hollerbaum & Schmidt,
Berlin
119 x 89 cm

No. 0093
Sven Brasch (1886-1970)
*Andreasen & Lachmann
Plakater*, 1912
Andreasen & Lachmann,
Copenhagen
89.5 x 62 cm

No. 0094
Julius E. F. Klinger
(1876-1950)
Künstler-Plakate, c. 1912
Hollerbaum & Schmidt,
Berlin
158 x 106 cm

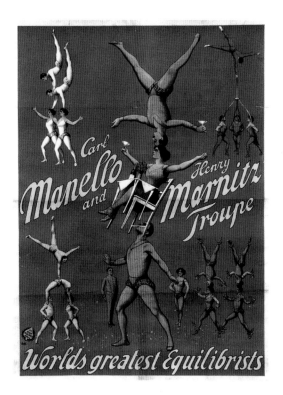

No. 0095

Artist unknown
*Carl Manello and Henry
Marnitz Troupe*, c. 1910
Lith. Adolpf Friedländer,
Hamburg
On linen, 70 x 94.5 cm

No. 0096

Artist unknown
Les Fluher, Cyclistes Sérieux
(poster for a bicycle
troupe), c. 1910
Lith. Adolph Friedländer,
Hamburg
On linen, 69 x 94 cm

No. 0097

Leonetto Cappiello
(1875-1942)
Maurin, 1906
Imp. P. Vercasson & Cie,
Paris
On linen, 116 x 158 cm

No. 0098

Hans Neumann (1888-1960)
Muki Schuhcrème (shoe
polish), c. 1915
Germany
66 x 98 cm

No. 0099

Raoul-Edward Hem
Aux Fabriques de Genève
(jewelry store), c. 1910
Affiches Kossuth, Paris
On linen, 119.5 x 160 cm

No. 0100

Fritz C. G. Rumpf
(1888-1949)
*Prince of Wales Schöne
Herren*, c. 1912
Curt Behrends, Berlin
On japan, 93.5 x 70.5 cm

No. 0101

Curt Vogt
F. M. Lenzner, Stettin
(poster for a packaging and
poster company), 1912
Germany
93.5 x 72 cm

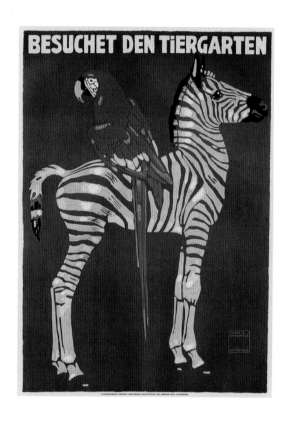

72

No. 0102
Ludwig Hohlwein
(1874-1949)
Besuchet den Tiergarten
(zoo poster), 1912
Wolfrum & Hauptmann,
Nuremberg, Germany
103 x 73 cm

No. 0103
Ludwig Hohlwein
(1874-1949)
*Zoölogischer Garten
München* (zoo poster), 1912
G. Schuh & Cie., Munich
125 x 91 cm

No. 0104
Olle Hjortzberg (1872-1959)
*Olympische Spiele
Stockholm 1912*, 1911
A. Bortzells Tr. A.B.,
Stockholm
101.5 x 74 cm

OLYMPISCHE SPIELE
~ STOCKHOLM 1912 ~
29 JUNI — 22 JULI

A. BÖRTZELLS TR. A. B. STOCKHOLM

74

No. 0105

Lucian Bernhard
(1883-1972)
Novelta Cigaretten, 1912
Hollerbaum & Schmidt,
Berlin
70 x 96 cm

No. 0106

Anna Soos Koranyi
(1870-1947)
*International Woman
Suffrage Congress*, 1913
Lith. Lengyel Lipüt,
Budapest
95.5 x 63 cm

No. 0107

Leopoldo Metlicovitz
(1868-1944)
Calzaturificio di Varese
(poster for a shoe
company), 1913
Off. G. Ricordi & C., Milan
141 x 101 cm

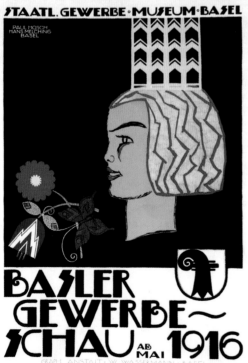

No. 0108

Saville Lumley (d.1950)
Daddy, what did YOU do in the Great War? 1914
Johnson, Riddel & Co.,
London
76 x 51 cm

No. 0109

Paul Hosch (1886-1955)
and Hans Melching
Basler Gewerbeschau 1916
(exhibition poster), 1916
Wassermann, Basel
On linen, 69.5 x 97.5 cm

No. 0110

Guy Dollian (b. 1887)
Sa bonne récompense
(movie poster), 1913
France
158.5 x 117 cm

No. 0111

Mihaly Bïro (1886-1948)
A Háboru Borzal Mai Ellen
(poster for the Hungarian
Social Democratic Party),
1912
Chromolith. Seidner,
Budapest
126.5 x 95 cm

78

No. 0112

Julius E. F. Gipkens
(1883-1969)
Der Gedeckte Tisch
(exhibition poster), 1912
Hollerbaum & Schmidt,
Berlin
95 x 69.5 cm

No. 0113

J. J. Chris Lebeau
(1878-1945)
Hamlet, c. 1915
Litho Lankhout, The
Hague, The Netherlands.
125.5 x 89 cm

No. 0114

Leon Bakst (1866-1924)
Caryathis (poster for a
dance recital), c. 1916
France
227 x 136 cm

No. 0115

Johann Baptist Maier
(Hans Ibe, 1881-1957)
Theater Electra, c. 1907
Schön & Maison, Munich
115 x 82.5 cm

No. 0116

Victor Cretem (1878-1966)
*2ᵉ Exposition d'Art
Décoratif*, 1917
J. Goffin, fils, Brussels
40.5 x 56 cm

No. 0117

Heinrich Leffler
(1863 -1919)
4. Kriegsanleihe (poster for
war loans), 1916
K.v.K. Hofl. J. Weiner,
Vienna
123.5 x 93.5 cm

No. 0118

Adrien Barrère (1877-1931)
Prince (movie poster),
c. 1912-3
Pathé Frères Editeurs,
Paris
159.5 x 119.5 cm

PRINCE

A. Barrère

PATHÉ FRÈRES ÉDITEURS

No. 0119

Ernst Deutsch (1887-1958)
English Club (menswear
shop), 1914
Verlag Atelier Deutsch,
Berlin
93 x 70.5 cm

No. 0120

Bart Anthony van der Leck
(1876-1958)
*Batavier-lijn Rotterdam-
Londen*, 1915
Geuze, Dordrecht, The
Netherlands
74 x 110 cm

No. 0121

Max Körner (b. 1887) and
W. Bühler (d. c.1917)
*Lutz' Detektiv & Kriminal-
Romane* (crime novels),
c. 1910
Emil Hochdanz, Stuttgart,
Germany
63 x 43 cm

No. 0122
Jupp Wiertz (1888-1939)
ACO Drahtlampe (lamp
wire), 1916
Kunstanstalt Weylandt,
Berlin
72 x 95.5 cm

I WANT YOU
FOR U.S. ARMY
NEAREST RECRUITING STATION

No. 0123
James Montgomery Flagg
(1887-1960)
I Want You for U.S. Army,
1917
USA
99.5 x 73.5 cm

No. 0124
John Warner Norton
(1876-1934)
Keep These Off the U.S.A.,
1918
The Strobridge Litho. Co.,
Cincinatti & New York
100 x 76 cm

No. 0125
Leendert (Leo) Gestel
(1881-1941)
Philips Arga Lamp, c. 1918
Van Leer, Amsterdam
78 x 102.5 cm

No. 0126
Boris M. Kustodiev
(1878-1927)
Liberty Loan, 1917
USSR
68 x 101 cm

No. 0127
Lucian Bernhard
(1883-1972)
Frauen! (poster for the
Committee of Women's
Associations of Germany),
1918
Werbedienst G.M.G.H.,
Berlin
68 x 95 cm

No. 0128
Walter Schnackenberg
(1880-1961)
Peter Pathe, Maria Hagen
(ballet poster), c. 1918
Kunstanstalt O. Consee,
Munich
123 x 90.5 cm

No. 0129
Oskar Schlemmer
(1888-1943)
*Ausstellung: Willy
Baumeister–Oscar
Schlemmer* (exhibition
poster), 1918
Kunsthaus Schaller,
Stuttgart, Germany
65 x 51 cm

KUNSTHAUS SCHALLER STUTTGART MARIENSTRASSE 14

AUSSTELLUNG: WILLY BAUMEISTER – OSKAR SCHLEMMER

90

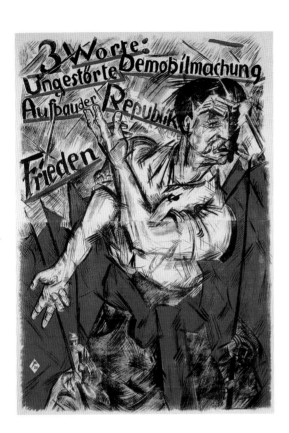

No. 0130

Theo Matejko (1893-1946)
Wählet Sozialdemokratisch
(Vote Social Democrat),
1919
Austria
95 x 120 cm

No. 0131

Hans Richter (1888-1976)
*3 Wörte: Demobilmachung,
Republik, Frieden*, 1919
Julius Sittenfeld, Berlin
140 x 96 cm

No. 0132

Cesar Klein (1876-1954)
Wer nicht Arbeitet (He who
is not working is digging
a grave for his children),
1919
Germany
122 x 86 cm

No. 0133
Bart Anthony van der Leck
(1876-1958)
Delftsche Slaolie, 1919
The Netherlands
89 x 59.5 cm

Final state of twelve
designs for a poster for the
Delft salad-oil company.
The design was turned
down in the board meeting
of the company and the
poster was never printed.

DE STIJL, CONSTRUCTIVISM, AND REVOLUTION

A 1914 poster for the Batavier Shipping Line by the Dutch artist Bart van der Leck displays an important step toward visual order, and the geometric partition of the composition can, in retrospect, be considered a precursor to De Stijl. The heavy black lines dividing the format suggest his earlier work in stained-glass design.

Many postwar Dutch posters display a discipline and organization inspired by De Stijl, one of the numerous iconoclastic reactions to the calamity of World War I. Launched at the end of 1917 by Theo van Doesburg and others, including the painter Piet Mondrian, De Stijl's primary goal was to purify art by discarding subject matter, illusion, decoration, and subjectivity, all of which De Stijl artists considered to be decadent and irrelevant features. A truly indigenous art movement, De Stijl is widely thought to be the most significant Dutch twentieth-century contribution to modern architecture, painting, and design.

In Russia, the revolution of October 1917 was deemed by many to be an opportunity for a new beginning in design. Posters played a major role, particularly during the reconstruction period that followed the Bolshevik victory in the civil war. Created for mainly uneducated audiences, the posters were considered especially important as propaganda tools to educate the masses regarding the virtues of the new Communist state. More consequential for the the course of graphic design in the twentieth century was the rise of Constructivism, exemplified by the architect, painter, photographer, and graphic designer El Lissitzky, an indefatigable visionary. He contended that artist/designer (or constructor as he preferred to be called) would unify art and technology by constructing a new world of objects that would benefit all mankind. He summarily relegated the subjective aesthetic experience and easel painting to the past. In 1921 Lissitzky traveled to Germany and the Netherlands, where his influence was strongly felt on the Bauhaus, De Stijl, and such nascent Dutch constructivists as Piet Zwart and Paul Schuitema.

Private motion picture companies in the Soviet Union were nationalized in 1923, and the brothers Georgii and Vladimir Augustovich Stenberg became the leading designers bringing Constructivist aesthetics to the new film posters. Their collaborative work was distinguished by a skillful manipulation of color and an unpredictable use of images. Their command of the lithographic printing process enabled them to exploit it beyond previous limitations. However, the primitive state of Soviet printing at the time made it difficult to print large photographic images, and for this reason the Stenbergs often drew their own illustrations by using a lantern projector to enlarge images from film negatives. These drawings were combined with flat color areas to express the essence of the film being promoted.

Throughout Europe, photomontage was increasingly becoming a popular medium and offered a method for merging incongruous images into Constructivist compositions. It became an incisive political weapon in the hands of designers such as John Heartfield in Germany. In the Soviet Union, the unrivaled master of this technique was Gustav Klutsis. Referring to the medium as "the art of construction for socialism," Klutsis was the genius of propaganda photomontage in the Soviet Union and skillfully exploited the poster as a means to extol Soviet accomplishments. He probably saw Heartfield's work when it was displayed in the Soviet Union during the 1930s, and his posters have often been compared to Heartfield's highly charged political statements. Klutsis considered photomontage to be the only legitimate modern poster medium and discarded all other means of social realism. While Klutsis consistently lauded the achievements of Stalin, his inflexible avant-garde approach ultimately led to his arrest during the purges in 1938, and he died in the Gulag in 1944.

94

No. 0134

Josef Fenneker (1895-1956)
*Das Ballett der Winter
Saison* (ballet poster), 1919
Plakatkunstanstalt Dinse &
Eckert, Berlin
140.5 x 95 cm

No. 0135

Cesar Klein (1876-1954)
Pelikan-Tinte (poster for ink
manufacturer), 1919
Günther Wagner, Hannover
and Vienna
61.5 x 50 cm

No. 0136

Walter Tiemann (1876-1951)
*Leipzig 1914, Internationale
Ausstellung für Buchgewerbe
und Graphik* (exhibition
poster), 1914
Germany
60 x 90 cm

No. 0137

Jan Theodoor Toorop
(1858-1928)
Pandorra (theater poster),
1919
S. Lankhout & Co., The
Hague, The Netherlands
113 x 84.5 cm

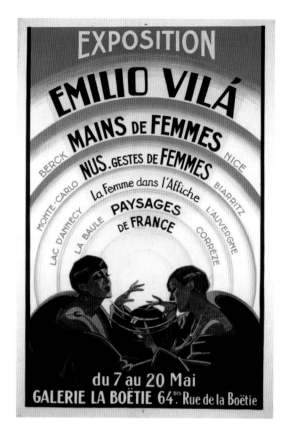

No. 0138
Charles Henri Honore
Loupot (1892-1962)
Plantol (soap), 1919
Switzerland
127 x 89 cm

No. 0139
Charles Henri Honore
Loupot (1892-1962)
Grieder (poster for a Zurich
silk merchant), 1919
Switzerland
128 x 91 cm

No. 0140
Emilio Vilá (1887-1967)
Exposition Emilio Vilá,
c. 1920
Paris
80 x 120 cm

No. 0141
Heinz Fuchs (1886-1961)
Arbeiter Hunger Tod naht
(Workers, hunger and
death draw near), 1919
Germany
104 x 74 cm

98

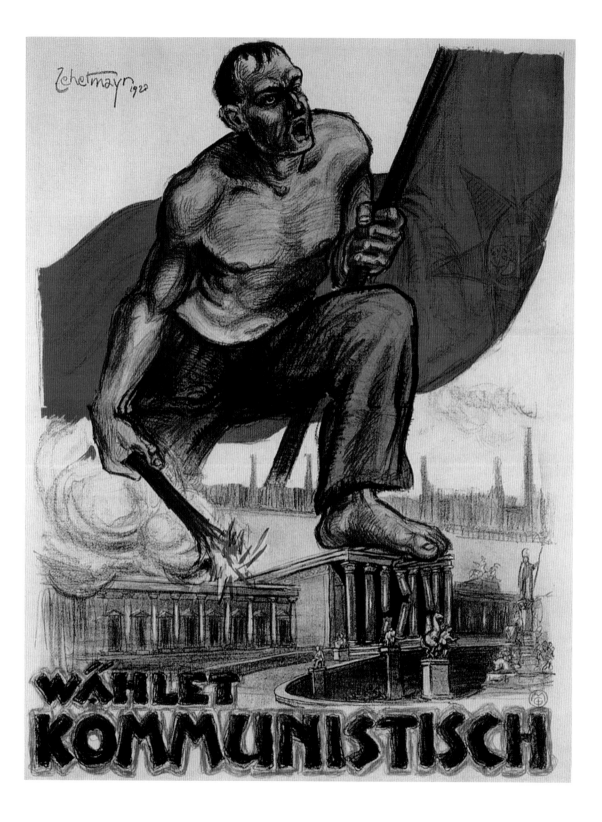

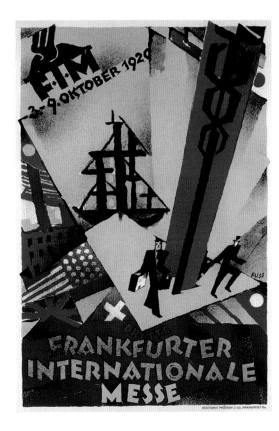

No. 0142

Hans Zehetmayr
Wählet kommunistisch (Vote
Communist), c. 1920
Druckerei M. G. I., Vienna
124 x 95.5 cm

No. 0143

Egge Sturm-Skria
(1894-1943)
Neve Vereinigung
(exhibition poster), c. 1920
A. Berger, Vienna
84 x 53 cm

No. 0144

Albert Fuss (1889-1969)
*Frankfurter internationale
Messe* (book fair poster),
1920
Wüsten & Co., Frankfurt,
Germany
75 x 51 cm

No. 0145

Bernd Steiner (1884-1933)
Wählt ChristlichSozial (Vote
Christian Socialist), 1920
Austria
125 x 94 cm

No. 0146
Burton Rice
See Him Through, 1918
American Lithographic Co.,
New York
On linen, 51 x 76 cm

No. 0147
Theo Matejko (1893-1946)
Der Galeeren-Sträfling
(movie poster), 1920
Waldheim-Eberle A. G.,
Vienna
185 x 126 cm

No. 0148
J. S. Brandoly
The Sensation of Davos,
c. 1920
Litho-Bruck Berlin-
Neukölln, Berlin
On linen, 141 x 94.5 cm

No. 0149
Artist unknown
Original Gutis (movie
poster), c. 1920
60.5 x 87 cm

102

IMP. J.E. GOOSSENS, S^{TÉ} A^{ME}, RUE HABERMAN, BRUXELLES.

No. 0150
Louis Raemaekers
(1899-1956)
L'Hecatombe la syphilis
(public health poster),
c. 1922
Imp. J. E. Goossens,
Brussels
118 x 78.5 cm

No. 0151
Pieter van der Hem
(1885-1961)
Indian Motorrijwielen
(motorcycles), c. 1920
Litho Lankhout, The
Hague, The Netherlands
108 x 72 cm

No. 0152
H. G. Brian de Kruyff van
Dorsser
*Lucht-Expres Holland-
Engeland*, c. 1921
Drukkerij Kotting,
Amsterdam
80 x 55 cm

No. 0153
Dudley Hardy (1867-1922)
The Yeomen of the Guard,
c. 1900-22
Waterlow & Sons, London
77 x 49 cm

104

No. 0154
Piet Zwart (1885-1977)
Laga Rubber-Vloeren
(poster for a rubber
flooring company), c. 1922
The Netherlands
91 x 65 cm

No. 0155
Artist unknown
Sun-Maid, 1922
J. Weiner Ltd., London
125 x 85 cm

No. 0156
Otto Baumberger
(1889-1961)
Marque PKZ (poster for a
menswear company), 1923
J. E. Wolfensberger, Zürich
127.5 x 89.5 cm

105

THEATRE DES CHAMPS-ELYSEES
6-23 MARS 1923
THEATRE KAMERNY DE MOSCOU
REPERTOIRE:
PHEDRE
ADRIENNE LECOUVREUR
SALOMEE
PRINCESSE BRAMBILLE
GIROFLEE GIROFLA
SOUS LA DIRECTION ARTISTIQUE D ALEXANDRE TAÏROFF
МОСКОВСКИЙ КАМЕРНЫЙ ТЕАТР
OEVRE DES CONSTRUCTIVISTES C.STENBERG W.STENBERG K.MEDUNEZKY MOSCOU 1923

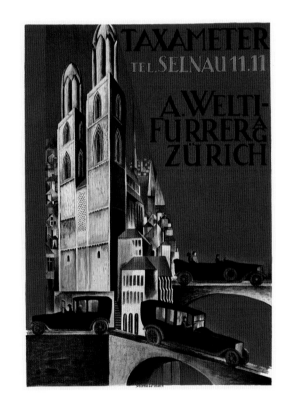

No. 0157

Stenberg Brothers (Georgii,
1900-1933, and Vladimir,
1899-1982) and Konstantin
Medunetsky (1899-1935)
*Theater Kamerny de
Moscou*, 1923
France
72 x 47 cm

No. 0158

Jules Isnard Dransy
(1883-1945)
Nicolas (poster for a chain
of wine shops), 1923
Poyet Frères, Paris
158 x 117.5 cm

No. 0159

Otto Morach (1896-1935)
Taxameter, 1923
J. E. Wolfensberger, Zürich
130 x 91 cm

No. 0160
Joost Schmidt (1893-1948)
Staatliches Bauhaus
(exhibition poster), 1923
Reineck & Klein, Weimar
68 x 48 cm

THE BAUHAUS AND THE NEW TYPOGRAPHY

On March 20, 1919, Walter Gropius officially opened the Staatliches Bauhaus in Weimar. Like most postwar modernists, the founders of the Bauhaus sought a new society that stressed a unity of art and craft. Graphic design was a decisive force, and formal design principles were stressed. After László Moholy-Nagy came to the Bauhaus, he acquired disciples like Herbert Bayer and Joost Schmidt who, as a student, designed the poster for the first Bauhaus exhibition in 1923. The Bauhaus helped to engender a revolution in typography and generated new typefaces, exemplified by Paul Renner's Futura in 1927. The Bauhaus moved to Dessau in 1927, and after seven resplendent years it was closed owing to the domination of the Dessau City Council by Nazis. A brief attempt to revive it in Berlin came to an end in 1933.

Many of the graphic design advances of the 1920s emerged from the Bauhaus and other modernist art movements, but these innovations were usually known to an exclusive audience. In the Netherlands, however, Jan Tschichold applied new design principles to commonplace design activities, educating a broad range of printers, typesetters, and typographers in their use. Originally trained as a traditional calligrapher, Tschichold was profoundly moved by the Bauhaus exhibition at Weimar in 1923, and he soon incorporated the concepts of the Bauhaus and the Soviet constructivists into his own work. Beginning in 1924, posters became one of his most important graphic-design mediums. From 1926 until 1928, his thirty-one posters for the Phoebus-Palast in Munich would rival the Stenbergs' work in the Soviet Union as paragons of film-poster design.

No. 0161
Herbert Bayer (1900-1985)
Europäisches Kunstgewerbe
(exhibition poster), 1927
Ernst Hedrich Nachf.,
Leipzig, Germany
90 x 60 cm

No. 0166

Jac Bieling
*Piano deklamatie zuang
L. V. A.* (concert poster),
c. 1925
The Netherlands
83.5 x 68.5 cm

No. 0167

Jan Wiegers (1893-1959)
Le Bœuf Sur Le Toit (ballet
poster), 1925
The Netherlands
Woodcut, 99.5 x 65 cm

No. 0168

Albert Johan Funke Küpper
(1894-1934)
Voorwaarts uw lichtbaak
M. A. Jacobson, Haarlem,
The Netherlands
117 x 84 cm

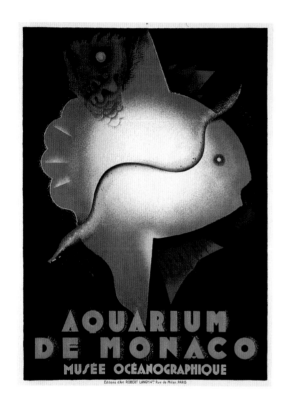

114

No. 0169
Jean George Leon Carlu
(1900-1997)
Aquarium de Monaco, 1926
Editions d'Art Robert Lang,
Paris
107.5 x 79 cm

No. 0170
Wout Schram (1895-1987)
Cleveland-Six (automobile
poster), c. 1925
Kunst en Arbeid,
Amsterdam
85.5 x 61.5 cm

No. 0171
Sybold van Ravesteyn
(1889-1983)
*Bezoekt de tentoonstelling
van Rekken's Huisvlijt*
(exhibition poster), c. 1925
The Netherlands
98.5 x 64 cm

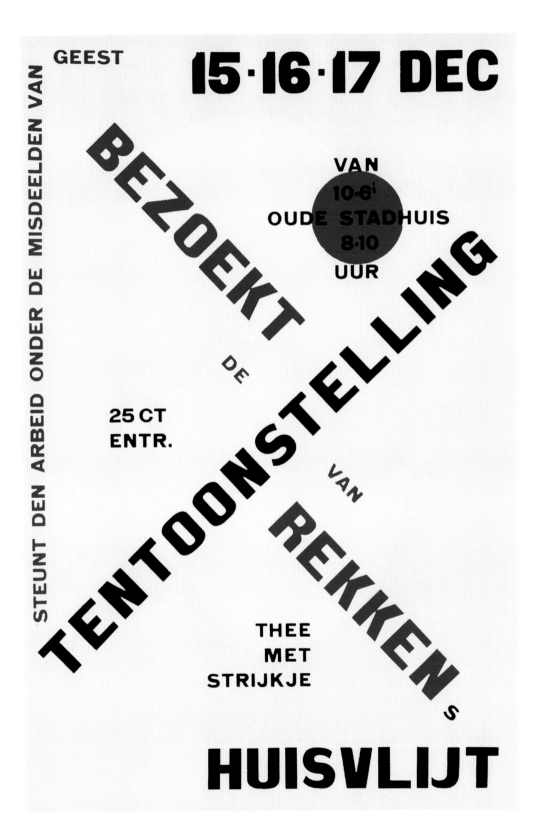

115

116

No. 0172
Charles Gesmar
(1900-1928)
Mistinguett (cabaret
poster), 1926
Imp. A. Chachoin, Paris
120.5 x 79 cm

No. 0173
Ernst Otto (1884-1967)
Wengen Schweiz (travel
poster), c. 1925
Switzerland
63 x 103 cm

No. 0174
Dolly Rudeman (1902-1980)
Potemkin (movie poster),
1926
The Netherlands
105 x 62 cm

118

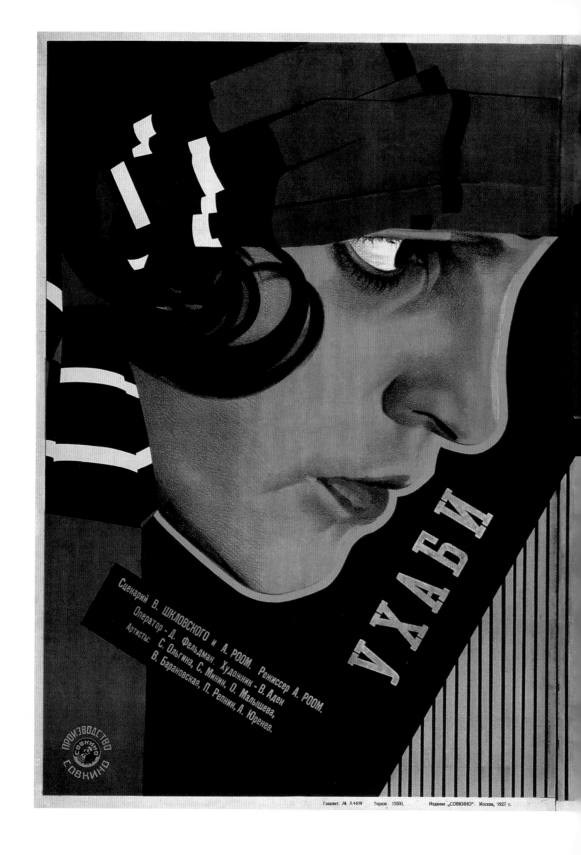

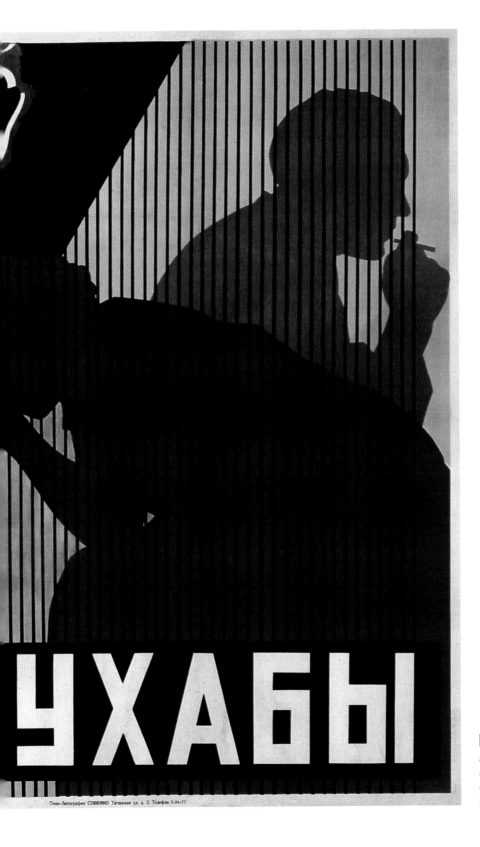

УХАБЫ

Типо-Литография СОВКИНО Таганская ул. д. 3. Телефон 2-24-77.

No. 0175
Artist unknown
Potholes (movie poster),
c. 1927
USSR

No. 0176

Ottomar Anton (1895-1976)
Nach Südamerika, c. 1925
Austria
70 x 105 cm

No. 0177

Stenberg Brothers (Georgii,
1900-1933, and Vladimir
1899-1982)
Buster Keaton, The General
(movie poster), 1929
USSR
105 x 70 cm

No. 0178

Nikolai P. Prousakov
(1900-1952) & Grigorii
Ilich Borisov (1899-1942)
A Journey to Mars (movie
poster), 1926
USSR
101.5 x 73 cm

No. 0179
Joseph (Jos) Rovers
(1893-1976)
*1928 IX Olympiade
Amsterdam*, 1927
Joh. Enschede & Zn,
Haarlem, The Netherlands
100 x 62 cm

No. 0180
Julius Ussy Engelhardt
(1883-1964)
Für den Wintersport (poster
for textile manufacturer),
1927
Klein & Volbert, Munich
119 x 93 cm

No. 0181
Jan Tschichold (1902-1974)
*Buster Keaton in "Der
General"* (movie poster:
The General), 1927
Germany
118.5 x 84 cm

No. 0182

Carl Otto Müller
(1901-1970)
*Elisabeth Bergner in Donna
Juana* (movie poster: *Doña
Juana*), c. 1927
Volk & Schreiber, Munich
119 x 85 cm

No. 0183

Jan Tschichold (1902-1974)
König Harlekin (movie
poster: *The Magic Flame*),
c. 1927
Germany
118.5 x 84 cm

No. 0184

Jan Tschichold (1902-1974)
*Die Kameliendame mit
Norma Talmadge* (movie
poster: *La Dame aux
Camélias*), 1927
Germany
118.5 x 84 cm

125

No. 0185
A. M. Cassandre
(1901-1968)
Étoile du Nord (railway
poster), 1927
Hachard & Cie., Paris
105 x 75.5 cm

ART DECO

Art Deco was the fashionable international style of the late 1920s and the early 1930s. Related to Art Nouveau, it arrived at a popular idiom that had its roots in Cubism, Futurism, the Vienna Secession, and Dada, as well as in Greek and Egyptian art. As opposed to the sumptuous approach of Art Nouveau, Art Deco reflected the industrial age with machine-based forms. The term Art Deco was actually coined in the 1960s by the English art historian Bevis Hillier, his source being the 1925 Exposition Internationale des Arts Décoratifs et Industriels Modernes in Paris.

Born as Jean-Maric Mouron in Kharkov, Ukraine, the Art Deco poster artist and type designer A. M. Cassandre arrived in Paris at the age of fourteen during World War I. From 1923 until 1936 he re-energized French advertising design through a remarkable series of posters. Familiarizing himself with the work of such artists as the Cubist painter Fernand Léger and the architect Le Corbusier, he applied their concepts to poster design. Cassandre possessed an extraordinary capacity to combine text and images into unified arrangements, and he attained succinct and powerful results by merging geometric shapes and simplified representational forms.

In the 1944 book *Language of Vision*, the designer and design historian György Kepes described Cassandre's method this way: "One unifying device employed by Cassandre was the use of a contour line common to various spatial units. The double outline takes on a double meaning, similar to a visual pun. It refers to inside and outside space simultaneously, . . . [and] the spectator is therefore forced into intensive participation as he seeks to resolve the apparent contradiction. But the equivocal contour line does more than unify different spatial data. It acts like a warp, weaving the threads of color planes into one rhythmical unity. The rhythmical flow of the line injects the picture surface with a sensual intensity."

In addition to Cassandre, many other graphic designers and illustrators incorporated concepts and images from Cubism in their work. The American-born Edward McKnight Kauffer was an important poster designer

who worked in England between World War I and World War II. His 131 posters for the London Underground reflected his deep understanding of Cubist painting.

The French artist Jean Carlu investigated the efficiency of communications in urban situations and carried out trials to test the legibility of posters going by spectators at different speeds. Paul Colin was the most productive French poster designer of his generation. He continued to design propaganda posters during World War II until France's surrender, and remained active until the early 1970s.

127

No. 0186

A. M. Cassandre
(1901-1968)
Nord Express (railway poster), 1927
Hachard & Cie., Paris
104.5 x 75 cm

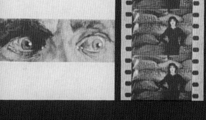

No. 0187

Piet Zwart (1885-1977)
ITF Film, 1928
M. V. v/h I Strang & Co.'s
Drukkerijen, The Hague,
The Netherlands
108 x 78 cm

No. 0188

Otto Baumberger
(1889-1961)
Forster Teil Ausverkauf
(poster for a carpet sale),
1928
Switzerland
128 x 90 cm

No. 0189

Willem Hendrik Gispen
(1890-1981)
Giso lampen, 1928
Kühn en Zn, Rotterdam,
The Netherlands
100 x 71 cm

No. 0190

Jupp Wiertz (1888-1939)
Deutschland, c. 1927
Germany
101 x 64 cm

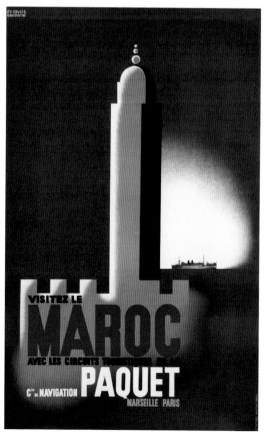

No. 0191

Hendrikus Theodorus
Wijdeveld (1885-1987)
*Stedelijk Museum
Amsterdam*, 1929
The Netherlands
65 x 51 cm

No. 0192

Francis Bernard (1900-1979)
Visitez le Morocco (travel
poster), 1930
France

No. 0193

A. M. Cassandre
(1901-1968)
*Automobiel & Motorrijwiel
Tentoonstelling* (automobile
exhibition), 1929
Nijgh en van Ditmar,
Rotterdam, The
Netherlands
113.5 x 81 cm

No. 0194

Semion Semionov
(1895-1972)
Who Are You? c. 1928
USSR
110 x 78.5 cm

132

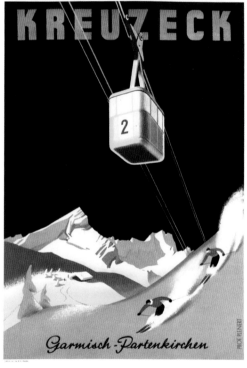

No. 0195
Paul Colin (1892-1986)
Théatre St. Georges, 1928
Imp. H. Chachoin, Paris
On linen, 39 x 59 cm

No. 0196
Prof. Plenert
Kreuzeck (travel poster),
c. 1935
Carl Lipp & Co, Munich
42 x 59.5 cm

No. 0197
Gaston Girbal (1888-1978)
Lorenza Margué, 1928
Paris
73 x 117 cm

No. 0198
Louis Oppenheim
(1879-1936)
S. Adam Pelzpflege (fur
storage company),
c. 1910
Selmar Bayer, Berlin
95 x 72 cm

No. 0199
Libis (H.B. Libiszewski,
1897-1985)
*Switzerland Alpine Postal
Motor Coaches*, 1930
J. C. Müller, Zürich
62 x 100 cm

134

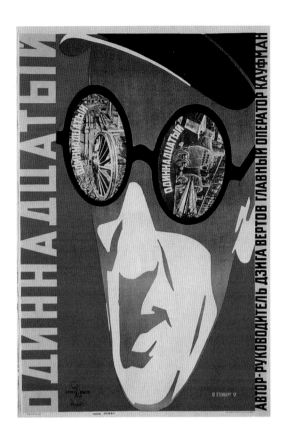

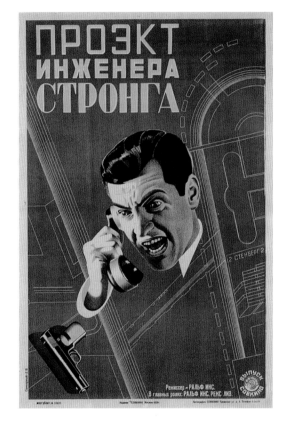

No. 0200

Stenberg Brothers (Georgii,
1900-1933, and Vladimir,
1899-1982)
The Miracle of the Wolves
(movie poster), c. 1927
USSR
105.5 x 76 cm

No. 0201

Stenberg Brothers (Georgii,
1900-1933, and Vladimir,
1899-1982)
*The Eleventh Year of the
Revolution* (movie poster),
1928
USSR
104.6 x 70.7 cm

No. 0202

Stenberg Brothers (Georgii,
1900-1933, and Vladimir,
1899-1982)
Engineer's Stroiga Project
(movie poster), 1929
USSR
105.5 x 76 cm

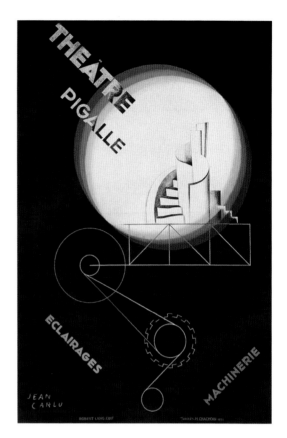

No. 0203

Jean George Leon Carlu
(1900-1997)
Théâtre Pigalle: Feu du ciel,
1929
Imp. Courbet, Paris
155 x 105 cm

No. 0204

Jean George Leon Carlu
(1900-1997)
*Théâtre Pigalle: Eclairages,
machinerie*, 1929
H. Chachoin, Paris
155 x 102 cm

No. 0205

Paul Colin (1892-1986)
André Renaud, 1929
H. Chachoin, Paris
159 x 113 cm

"Succès" 7, imp." Marie Blanche, Paris. H. CHACHOIN imp. 1929

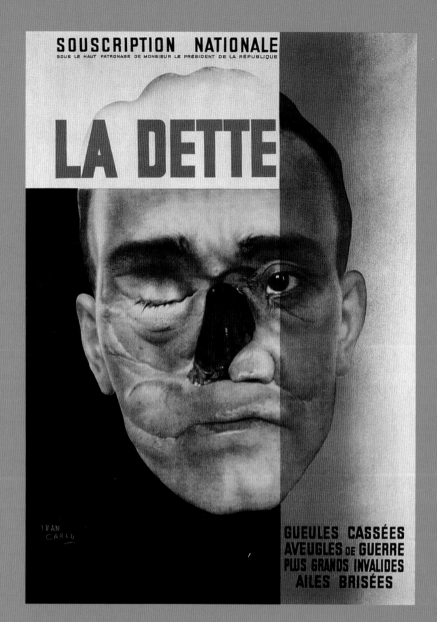

138

No. 0206
Jean George Leon Carlu
(1900-1997)
La dette (poster for a lottery
to benefit war veterans),1931
France
106 x 75 cm

CONSTRUCTIVISM VERSUS EXPRESSIONISM

As in many parts of the world, the 1930s in Europe presented a disheartening picture. Uncertain and worsening economic and political conditions erased the optimism and idealism of the 1920s, and as National Socialism became the dominant force in Germany, conditions became progressively more uncomfortable for the artistic avant-garde. Energizing international contacts occurred less frequently, and a mood of gloomy isolation began to be prevalent among those in the arts. Although the European social order remained fundamentally intact during the 1930s, it became more splintered as the world depression continued unabated, bringing with it increased unemployment and a breakdown of trade.

As the debilitating political and economic situation took hold, a new realism in painting arose as a counter-reaction to Constructivism. Against the expectation that security could be secured through better technology, there arose a growing skepticism, which was gradually transformed into feelings of indifference and despondency. This was exemplified by Surrealism, a movement that sanctioned a submission to the subconscious and a cynicism regarding the inconsistent values of an unstable society. Architecture also began to display a reactionary trend. Graphic design did not remain unscathed. Profuse decoration began to reappear, and traditional illustration started to regain some of the territory it had ceded to photography.

The Nazi ascendancy in Europe prompted many intellectuals, scientists, writers, architects, and artists to immigrate to the United States during the late 1930s. After the Nazis closed the Bauhaus in 1933 many faculty members and students left Germany. The architects Gropius, Ludwig Mies van der Rohe, and Marcel Breuer brought functionalist architectural to the United States, and Bayer and Moholy-Nagy brought with them modernist graphic design ideas. Other European graphic designers who moved to the United States included Will Burtin, Jean Carlu, George Giusti, and Herbert Matter.

No. 0207
G. Paul H. Schuitema
(1897-1973)
Centrale Bond 30,000
Transportarbeiders (union
poster), 1930
The Netherlands
115.5 x 75.5 cm

140

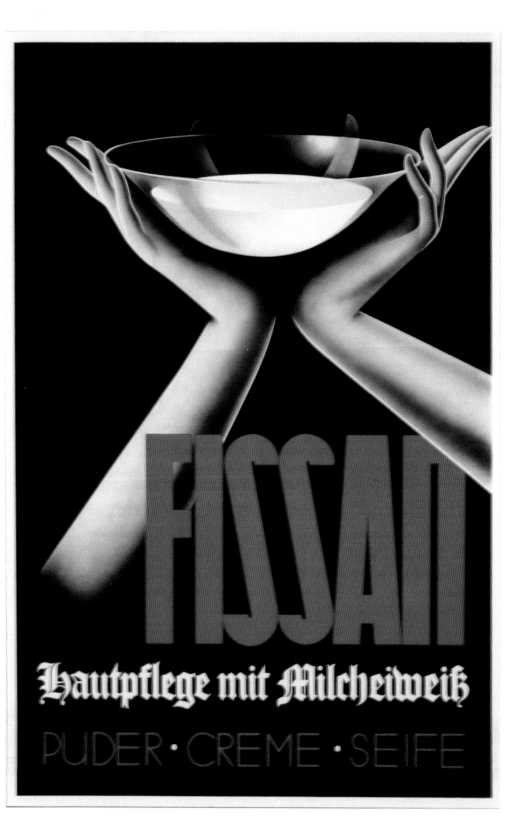

No. 0208

Joseph Binder (1897-1991)
*Fissan Hautpflege mit
Milcheiweiss* (skin-care
product), c. 1930
Germany
52 x 72 cm

No. 0209

Artist unknown
Mediterranean New-York,
c. 1930
France
63.5 x 101.5 cm

No. 0210

Artist unknown
Deen, Le Demon Rouge
(poster for a daredevil
motorcycle show), c. 1930
France
62 x 85 cm

No. 0211

C. Villot
Au Grand Pasteur, c. 1930
Imp. Générale, Grenoble,
France
120 x 159 cm

142

No. 0215
A. M. Cassandre
(1901-1968)
Triplex (manufacturer
of safety glass for
automobiles), 1931
Alliance Graphique
Loupot–Cassandre, Paris
120 x 80 cm

No. 0216
Ch. Yray
Pélican Cigarettes, c. 1930
Aff. Edia, Paris
60 x 80 cm

No. 0217
Jacobus (Koos) Hooykaas
(1903-1969)
De Rotterdamsche Byenkorf
(a department store
in Rotterdam), 1930
Steendruk Flach, Sneek,
The Netherlands
114.5 x 82 cm

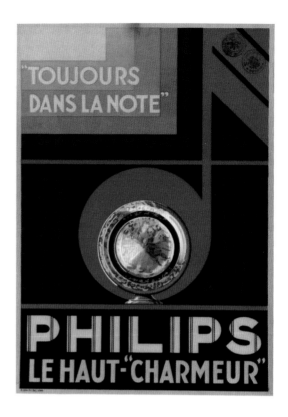

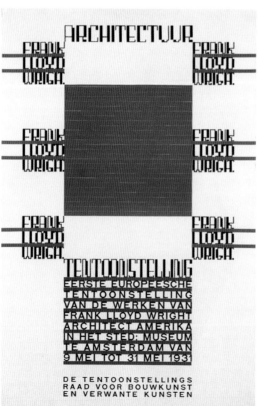

No. 0218

Léo Marfurt (1894-1977)
Minerva (automobile
poster), 1931
Les Créations Publicitaires,
Brussels
160.5 x 119 cm

No. 0219

Hendrikus Theodorus
Wijdeveld (1885-1987)
*Architectuur Tentoonstelling
Frank Lloyd Wright*, 1931
Letterpress Joh. Enschedé
& Zonen, Haarlem, The
Netherlands
77 x 49.5 cm

No. 0220

Emmanuel Gaillard
*Philips: Le haute–
"charmeur,"* c. 1930
31 x 43 cm

No. 0221

Gustav Gustavovic Klutsis
(1895-1944)
*The USSR is the Avant-Garde
of the World Proletariat*,
1931
USSR
144 x 104 cm

145

146

AEROS

LUBRICA

THE ARISTOCRAT

No. 0222
Edward McKnight Kauffer
(1890-1954)
Aero Shell, 1932
Chorley & Pickersgill Ltd.,
Leeds, UK
76.5 x 113 cm

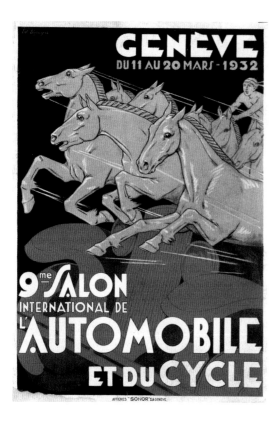

148

No. 0223

Edouard Elzingre
(1880-1966)
*9me Salon International de
Automobile*, c. 1930
Affiches "Sonor," Geneva
91.5 x 128 cm

No. 0224

Ludwig Hohlwein (1874-1949)
*Erster Nationalsozialistischer
Reichsjugendtag* (poster for
Nazi Youth Day), 1932
Herm. Sonntag & Co.,
Munich
85.5 x 120 cm

No. 0225

Artist unknown
Goldbar Cigarettes
China
Metal strips, 28 x 78 cm

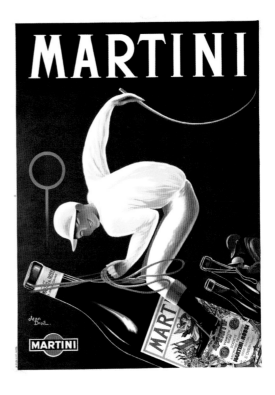

No. 0226
Frans Waslander
(1913-1977)
Fotomontage en Fotokunst
(poster for a lecture by Piet
Zwart), 1931
The Netherlands
92.5 x 71.5 cm

No. 0227
John Heartfield (1891-1968)
*Kämpfe mit der
Kommunistischen Partei!*
(Communist Party election
poster), 1932
Uranus-Druckerei
G.m.b.H., Berlin
100.5 x 70.5 cm

No. 0228
Jean Droit (1884-1961)
Martini, c. 1930
France
59.5 x 81 cm

No. 0229
Victor Koretsky
(1909-1998)
Under Lenin's Banner, 1932
USSR
120 x 84.5 cm

No. 0230
Artist unknown
*Let's Build a Fleet of
Airships for Lenin*, 1931
USSR
74 x 104 cm

No. 0231
Gustav Gustavovic Klutsis
(1895-1944)
*In Our Country the Victory
of Socialism is Guaranteed*,
1932
USSR
145x102 cm

No. 0232
Johannes Bernardus
Romein (Bert) (1894-1957)
Rynbende's Schiedam,
c. 1932
Van Leer & Co., Amsterdam
140 x 90 cm

No. 0233
Hermann Alfred Koelikker
(1894-1965)
Sissa, 1932
J. C. Müller, Zürich
127.5 x 90 cm

No. 0234
Atelier Lumax
Jeugd Werkloozendienst
(poster for youth camps),
c. 1932
The Netherlands
74.5 x 49.5 cm

No. 0235
S. D. Pomaiotaky
Hong Kong, c. 1932
Asiatic Printing Press,
Hong Kong
108 x 78.5 cm

153

No. 0238
Gustav Gustavovic Klutsis
(1895-1944)
Hail to the Worldwide
October Celebration, 1933
USSR
159.5 x 103 cm

No. 0239
Francis Bernard (1900-1979)
Air Oriënt, c. 1932
Editions Paul Martial, Paris
99 x 62 cm

No. 0240
Helmuth Kurtz (1903-1959)
Single Shell, c. 1932
Switzerland
98.5 x 54.5 cm

No. 0241
Andreas K. Hemberger
B. M. W., 1933
Kunst im Druck, Munich
102.5 x 74.5 cm

No. 0242
Anders and Per Beckman
(Anders, 1907-1967, and
Per, 1913-1989)
Swedish Air Lines,1932
Sweden

No. 0243
Munetsugu Satomi
(1900-1995)
K.L.M., 1933
The Netherlands
99 x 61.5 cm

No. 0244
Max Bill (1908-1994)
Single Shell, c. 1933
Gebr. Fretz, Zürich
100 x 55.5 cm

160

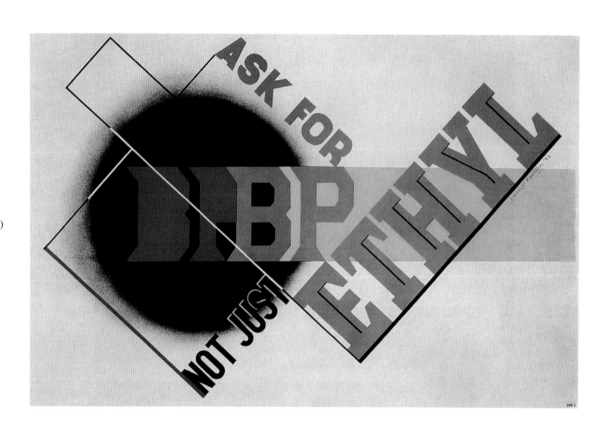

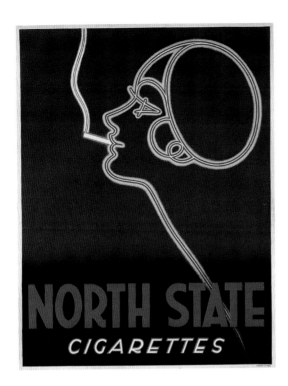

No. 0245
Edward McKnight Kauffer
(1890-1954)
Ask for BP, Not Just Ethyl,
1933
UK
74.5 x 112 cm

No. 0246
Carati
North State Cigarettes, 1933
Rotterdam, The Netherlands
117.5 x 89.5 cm

No. 0247
Johann Walther (Gene
Walter) (1910-1968)
KNSM, 1933
De Bussy, Amsterdam
100 x 62.5 cm

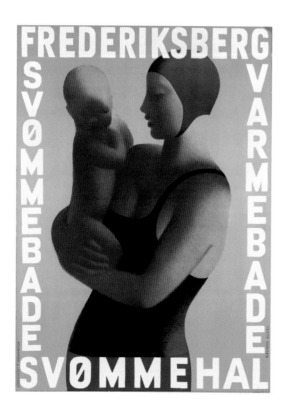

No. 0248
Henri C. Pieck (1895-1972)
Jaarbeurs Utrecht (fair
poster), 1934
The Netherlands
99.5 x 73 cm

No. 0249
Aage Sikker Hansen
(1897-1955)
Frederiksberg Svømmehal
(swimming pool), 1934
Denmark

No. 0250
Artist unknown
*Marlene Dietrich in "Song
of Songs"* (movie poster),
c. 1933
Mes & Bronkhorst, Haarlem,
The Netherlands
99 x 63 cm

No. 0251
Herbert Matter (1907-1984)
Svizzera (travel poster),
1934
Switzerland
102 x 64 cm

163

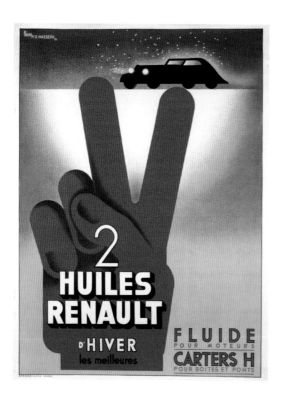

164

No. 0252
Pierre Fix-Masseau
(1905-1994)
2 Huiles Renault (poster for
motor oil), 1934
France
84 x 114 cm

No. 0253
Henri Fehr (1890-1974)
*XI Salon Internationale de
l'Automobile*, 1934
Affiches "Sonor," Geneva
90 x 127.5 cm

No. 0254
Zulla
Liquer Izarra, 1934
France
80 x 120 cm

No. 0255
Otto Baumberger
(1889-1961)
The Electric Simplon Line,
1933
Fretz Bros. Ltd., Zurich,
Switzerland
On linen, 64 x 101.5 cm

No. 0256
Victor J. Desmeure
*Internationale Koloniale
Ausstellung*, 1931
Robert Lang Éditeur, Paris
On linen, 62 x 100 cm

No. 0257
Ricard Fàbregas
(1906-1947)
Smoking (cigarette papers),
c. 1935
Llauger, Barcelona
47 x 67 cm

166

No. 0258
Artist unknown
Plaza Toros de Granada
(bullfight poster), 1935
Imprento de Torerias,
Madrid
55.5 x 80 cm

No. 0259
Max Ponty (1904-1972)
Chamonix (travel poster),
1936
Switzerland
On linen, 62 x 100 cm

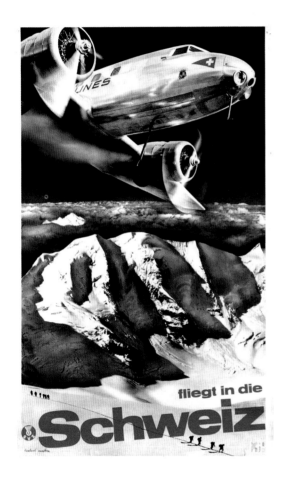

167

No. 0260

Herbert Matter
(1907-1984)
Fliegt in die Schweiz (travel
poster), 1935
Switzerland
64 x 103 cm

No. 0261

Alfred Mahlau (1894-1967)
Finland (travel poster),
1929
H. G. Rahtgens, Lübeck,
Germany
101 x 62 cm

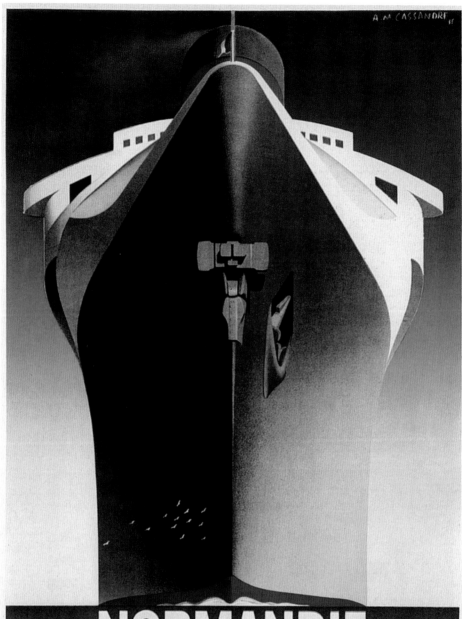

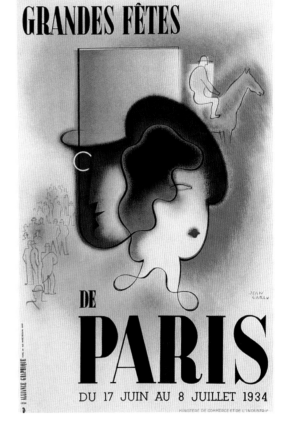

No. 0262
A. M. Cassandre
(1901-1968)
Normandie, 1935
L. Danel, Lille, France
100 x 62.5 cm

No. 0263
Hans Neuburg (1904-1983)
Photo: Anton Stankowksi
Super Bouillon Liebig, 1934
Ringer & Co., Zofingen,
Switzerland
127 x 90 cm

No. 0264
Jean George Leon Carlu
(1900-1997)
Grande Fêtes de Paris, 1934
Alliance Graphique, Paris
95.5 x 63 cm

No. 0265
Herbert Matter
(1907-1984)
*All Roads Lead to
Switzerland*, 1935
Switzerland
101 x 63.5 cm

No. 0266
Xanti (Alexander
Schawinsky) (1904-1979)
SI (propaganda poster for
Benito Mussolini), 1934
Alfieri e Lacroix, Milan
96.5 x 66.5 cm

No. 0267
Maria Weninger Emmerich
(1909-1977)
Der Bunte Schleier (movie
poster: *The Painted Veil*),
1936
Waldheim-Eberle, Vienna
278 x 123.5 cm

172

No. 0268
Herbert Matter
(1907-1984)
Pontresina (travel poster),
1936
Tiefdruck Conzett & Huber,
Zürich
102 x 63.5 cm

No. 0269
Ingrid Louisa Bade
(1908-1989)
Finnland (travel poster for
Finnish Railways), 1936
F. Tilgmann, Finland
100 x 62 cm

No. 0270
Munetsugu Satomi
(1900-1995)
Travel N.Y.K. Line, 1936
Kyodo Printing Co., Japan
91.5 x 63.5 cm

No. 0271
Etienne Clare (1901-1975)
Thun Lido (travel poster),
1936
Lith. Casserini Aebi Thun,
Switzerland
64 x 100 cm

No. 0272 / No. 0273
Pièrre Bellenger (b. 1909)
Quinquina Bourin, 1936
Etbts. de la Basselai, Paris
On linen, 124.5 x 200 cm

No. 0274
Mark S. Severin
(1906-1987)
Ostende-Dover, 1934
L.F. de Vos & Co., Antwerp,
Belgium
62 x 100 cm

No. 0275
Leblanc
Kovacs Lajos, 1934
65 x 100 cm

No. 0276
Artist unknown
*Oil Industry at the Black
Sea*, 1936
Turkey
On linen, 66 x 95.5 cm

No. 0277
Gustav G. Klutsis
(1895-1944)
*Be Proud, Be Happy to
Become a Soldier in the Red
Army*, 1936
USSR
63 x 95 cm

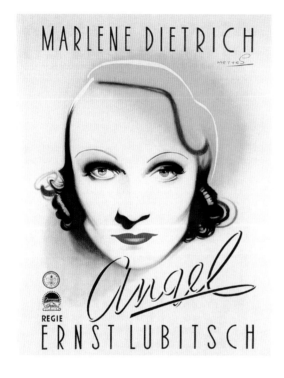

No. 0278

Frans J. E. Mettes (1909-1984)
Angel (movie poster), 1937
The Netherlands
80 x 62 cm

No. 0279

Arjen Galema (1886-1974)
Begeerte (movie poster: *Desire*), 1936
Luii & Co., Amsterdam
99.5 x 71 cm

No. 0280

Hans Virtus Vierthaler (1910-1942)
Entartete Kunst (poster for Nazi exhibition of modern art), 1936
Max Schmidt & Söhne, Munich
120 x 86 cm

ENTARTETE KUNST

ausstellung von „kulturdokumenten" des bolschewismus und jüdischer zersetzungsarbeit. vom 4. III. bis 31. III. 1936

was wir in dieser interessanten schau sehen, wurde einmal ernst genommen !!!!!

vierthaler

Druck: Max Schmidt & Söhne, München

Ausstellung im Weißen Saal der Polizeidirektion, Neuhauserstraße, Eingang Augustinerstraße
Geöffnet: Werktags von 10 bis 21 Uhr, Sonntags 10 bis 18 Uhr
Eintritt: Für Einzelpersonen 20 Pfennig. Bei geschlossenen Führungen der Betriebe 10 Pfennig.
Anmeldung der Führungen im Gauamt der N.S.-Gem. „Kraft durch Freude" Abt. Propaganda

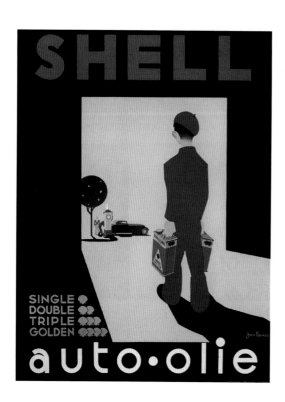

No. 0281
Charles Henri Honore
Loupot (1892-1962)
St. Raphaël, 1937
Joseph-Charles, Paris
156 x 115 cm

No. 0282
Jan Frederik Lavies
(1902-2004)
Shell, c. 1936
Offsetdruk J. Smulders &
Co., The Hague,
The Netherlands
118.5 x 88 cm

No. 0283

László Moholy-Nagy
(1895-1946)
*Quickly Away, Thanks to
Pneumatic Doors*, 1936
Waterlow & Sons, Ltd.,
London and Dunstable
101.5 x 63.5 cm

No. 0284

Hiromu Hara (att.)
(1903-1986)
Nikke, c. 1937
Japan
77 x 52.5 cm

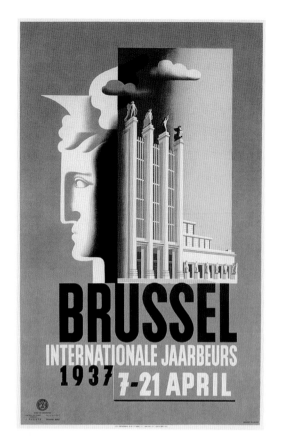

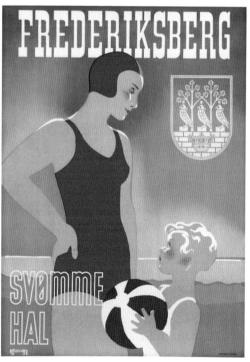

No. 0285

Léo Marfurt (1894-1977)
Brussel Internationale Jaarbeurs (fair poster), 1937
Les Créations Publicitaires, Brussels
99.5 x 62 cm

No. 0286

Thor Bögelund (1890-1959)
Frederiksberg, 1938
Andreasen & Lachmann, Denmark
On linen, 62 x 85.5 cm

No. 0287

Artist unknown
Porque?, 1937
Subsecretaria de Propaganda, Spain
100 x 68.5 cm

No. 0288

Lucian Bernhard (1883-1972)
Rem, 1937
USA
113.5 x 151.5 cm

182

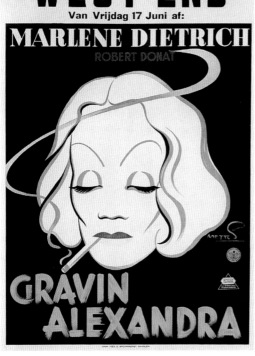

No. 0289

Paul Colin (1892-1986)
Paris Exposition Internationale, 1937
France
c. 110 x 70 cm

No. 0290

Frans J. E. Mettes (1909-1984)
Gravin Alexandra (movie poster), 1938
Mes & Bronkhorst Haarlem, The Netherlands
100 x 65.7 cm

No. 0291

Agullo
Madrilenos! Catalonia os ama, 1937
Graf. Ultra, Barcelona
110 x 76 cm

No. 0292
Alois Carigiet (1902-1985)
Graubünden, Schweiz: Das Ferien Paradeis (travel poster), 1937
Switzerland

No. 0293
Edward McKnight Kauffer
(1890-1954)
ARP, 1938
HMSO, London

No. 0294
Barnett Freedman
(1901-1958)
Circus, 1937
London Transport Executive
Two sheets

185

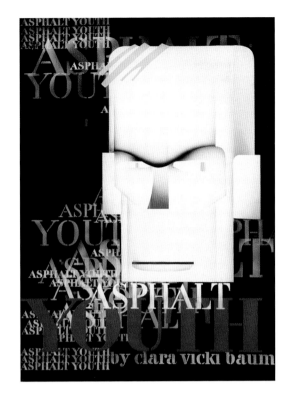

No. 0295
Jan Tschichold (1902-1974)
Der Berufsphotograph
(exhibition poster), 1938
Benno Schwabe, Basel,
Switzerland
63 x 89 cm

No. 0296
Jan Frederik Lavies
(1902-2004)
Essolube, c. 1938
Kühn & Zn, Rotterdam,
The Netherlands
108 x 83 cm

No. 0297
Johannes Bernardus (Bert)
Romein (1894-1957)
Asphalt Youth, c. 1938
The Netherlands
120 x 80 cm

No. 0298
Hermann Kosel (1896-1983)
Südbahn Hotel, c. 1938
Christoph Reisser's Söhne,
Vienna
61 x 93 cm

188

No. 0299
Jean Luc
Monaco Aquarium, 1939
Imprimerie Sic, Monaco
63 x 98 cm

No. 0300
Franz Würbel (b. 1896)
Olympische Spiele, 1936
Germany, 62.5 x 101 cm

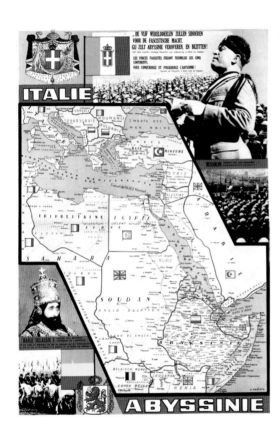

189

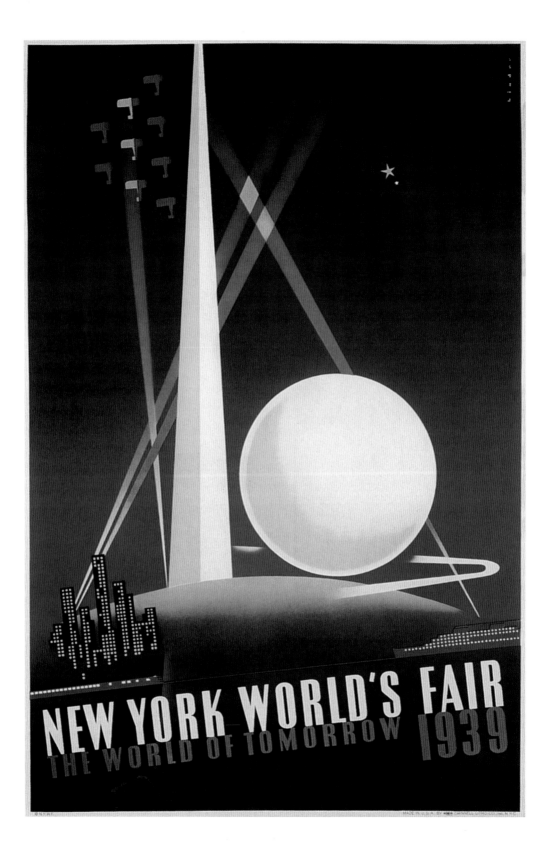

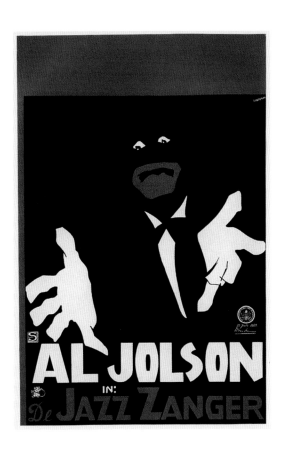

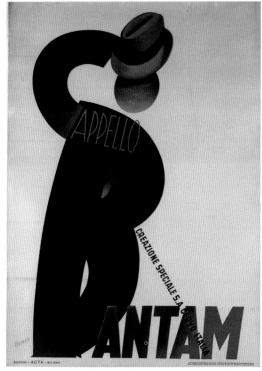

No. 0304

Joseph Binder (1898-1972)
New York World's Fair, 1939
Grinnell Litho. Co.,
New York
76 x 50.5 cm

No. 0305

Dolly Rudeman (1902-1980)
Al Jolson in De Jazz Zanger
(movie poster), 1928
Strang & Co., The Hague,
The Netherlands
92.5 x 60.5 cm

No. 0306

Artist unknown
Finland, c. 1938
Finland
c. 100 x 62 cm

No. 0307

Gino Boccasile (1901-1952)
Cappello Bantam (poster
for a hat company), 1938
R. Questura di Milano,
Milan
100 x 139 cm

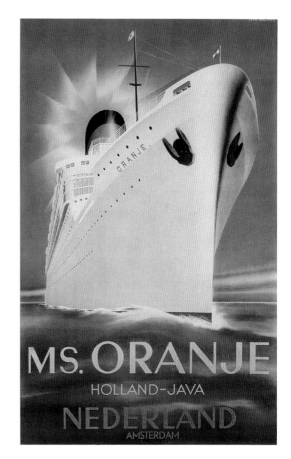

No. 0308
Artist unknown
Ein Folk, ein Reich, ein Führer! (One People, One Nation, One Leader), 1938
Offsetdruck Carl Werner, Reichenbach, Germany
83.5 x 59 cm

No. 0309
Johann Walther (Gene Walter) (1910-1968)
MS. Oranje, c. 1939
The Netherlands
98.5 x 60.5 cm

No. 0310
Zakj
Egyptian State Railways, 1938
Egypt
99 x 68 cm

194

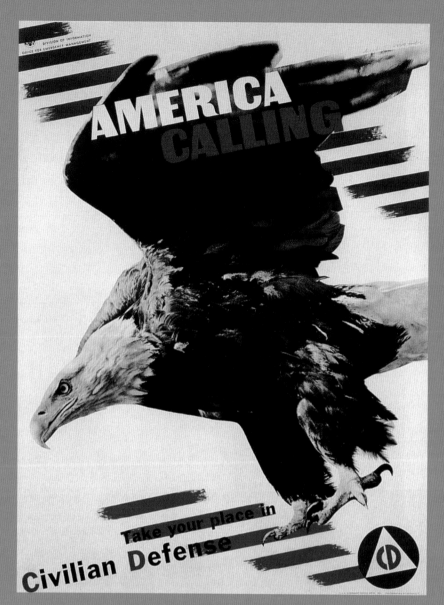

No. 0311
Herbert Matter (1907-1984)
Photo: Arthur H. Fisher
America Calling, 1941
U.S. Government Printing
Office, Washington, D.C.
102 x 75 cm

WORLD WAR II

During World War II, the poster again became an essential propaganda medium, playing a major role in the struggle for public support of the war effort in all nations involved in the conflict. The United States maintained an energetic propaganda campaign, encouraging Americans to enlist, buy war bonds, and work in industry. Many painters, illustrators, and graphic designers were commissioned by the U.S. Office of War Information and, in addition to other printed material, produced a wide range of posters to support America's war effort.

In 1941, Jean Carlu was commissioned to design, the well-known "America's answer! Production" poster. In this Art Deco–inspired design a stolid gloved hand with a wrench tightens a bolt, the first "O" of the word "production." The printed edition exceeded one-hundred thousand copies and resulted in Carlu being honored by the New York Art Director's Club. Herbert Bayer's posters produced during and following World War II were far more illustrative than the Constructivist designs of his Bauhaus period.

195

No. 0312

Jean George Leon Carlu
(1900-1997)
*America's Answer!
Production*, 1941
U.S. Government Printing
Office, Washington, D.C.
102 x 76 cm

ЗАЩИТА ОТЕЧЕСТВА ЕСТЬ СВЯЩЕННЫЙ Д

КАЖДОГО ГРАЖДАНИНА СССР!

No. 0313
Victor Koretsky
(1909-1998)
*Defense of the Fatherland
is the Sacred Duty of Every
Citizen of the USSR*, 1941
USSR
69.5 x 105.5 cm

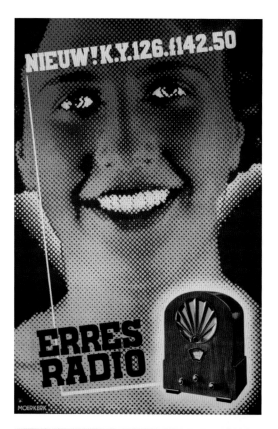

No. 0314
Johan Marie Moerkerk
(1903-1988)
Erres Radio, c. 1940
The Netherlands
76 x 117 cm

No. 0315
Johannes Handschin
(1899-1948)
Indiana Stumpen (cigars),
1940
Germany
On cardboard, 50 x 70 cm

No. 0316
Carlo L. Vivarelli
(1919 -1986)
Flums Grossberg, 1940
Sarganserländische
Buchdruckerei, Mels and
Flums, Switzerland
70 x 100 cm

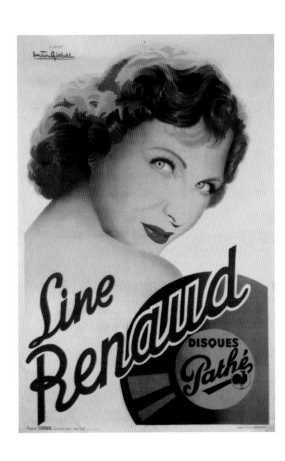

No. 0317
Gaston Girbal (1888-1978)
Line Renaud, c. 1940
France
80 x 119 cm

No. 0318
Krautschneider
Meinl Kaffee, c. 1940
F. Adametz, Vienna
45 x 60 cm

No. 0319
Otto Exinger
Zur Stärkung, c. 1940
F. Adametz, Vienna
45 x 60 cm

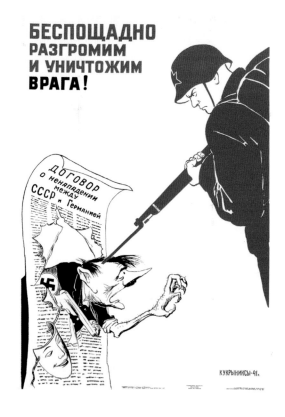

No. 0320
Artist unknown
*Glory to the Partisan
Heroes, Who Destroy the
Fascist Hinterland*, 1941
USSR
60 x 93.5 cm

No. 0321
Artist unknown
*Eliminate the Fascist
Saboteurs Mercilessly*, 1941
USSR
84 x 63.5 cm

No. 0322
Kukryniksi Group (Mikhail
Kuprianov, Porfiri Krylov,
and Nikolai Sokolov)
*We Shall Mercilessly Defeat
and Eliminate the Enemy*,
1941
USSR
62 x 88 cm

No. 0323
Artist unknown
Me 109, 1941
101 x 71 cm

No. 0324
Werner von Axster-
Heudtlass
Bordfünker der Luftwaffe,
c. 1940
Germany
42 x 59 cm

202

KEEP 'EM ROLLING!

DIVISION OF INFORMATION
OFFICE FOR EMERGENCY MANAGEMENT
WASHINGTON, D.C.

No. 0325
Leo Lionni (1910-1999)
Keep 'em Rolling!, 1941
Office for Emergency
Management, Washington,
D.C.

No. 0326
Alois Carigiet (1902-1985)
Blanc (shop poster), c. 1940
Geneva

No. 0327
Pierre Gauchat (1902-1956)
*Macht Ferien Schafft
Arbeit!*, 1940
Swiss Tourist Board

No. 0328
Artist unknown
Twelve billion yen savings
campaign poster, 1940
Japan
76 x 52 cm

No. 0329
F. H. K. Henrion (1914-1990)
Untitled, 1943
U.S. Office of War
Information, London

No. 0330
Jean George Leon Carlu
(1900-1997)
Give 'em Both Barrels, 1941
Office of Emergency
Management,
Washington, D.C.
On linen, 101.5 x 77 cm

No. 0331
Fritz Bühler (1909-1963)
Union (poster for a fuel
company), 1943
Zürich

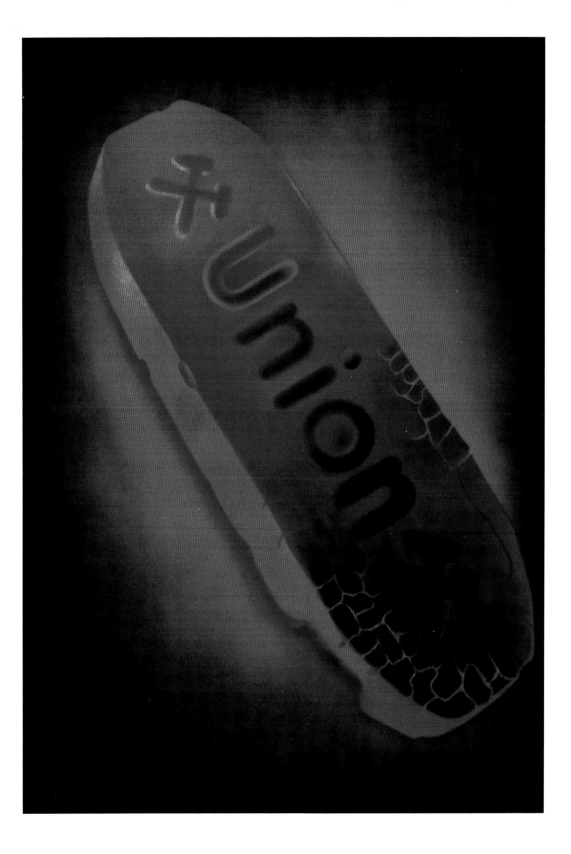

MELDT U ALS
OORLOGSVRIJWILLIGER
LAND · ZEE · LUCHT

206

No. 0332

Pat Keely (d.1970)
*Meldt u als
Oorlogsvrijwilliger* (Join the
War Volunteers), 1944
HMSO, London, on
behalf of the Free Dutch
Government

No. 0333

Pat Keely (d.1970)
Indie Moet Vrij! (Liberate
the East Indies), 1944
HMSO, London, on
behalf of the Free Dutch
Government

No. 0334

Hans Neuburg (1904-1983)
*Das Internationale Komitee
vom Roten Kreuz hilft*, 1944
Switzerland

No. 0335

Abram Games (1914-1996)
*Exposition des Armees
Britanniques*, 1945
Paris

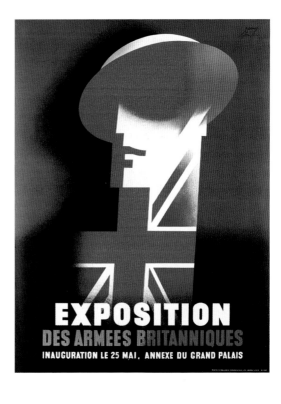

208

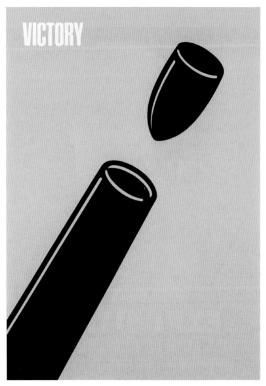

No. 0336
Lewitt-Him (Jan Lewitt,
1907-1991, and George
Him, 1900-1982)
Food Needs Transport, 1944
UK

No. 0337
Shigeo Fukuda (1932-2009)
Victory, 1975
Japan

No. 0338
Ib Andersen (1907-1969)
DDL, 1945
Denmark

210

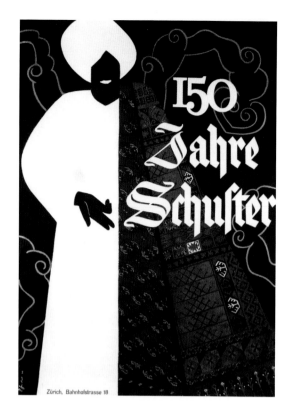

No. 0339
Paul Erkelens (b. 1919)
Homeward, 1944
The Netherlands
60 x 100 cm

No. 0340
Pierre Gauchat (1902-1956)
150 Jahre Schuster (poster
for a carpet company),
1945
Orell Füssli, Zürich
90 x 128 cm

211

No. 0341
Herbert Leupin (1916-1999)
Steinfels (poster for
cleaning powder), 1944
Wassermann, Basel
90 x 128 cm

No. 0342
Aage Lundvald (att.)
King Kong (movie poster),
c. 1945
Rasmussen Nilsson,
Denmark
64 x 85.5 cm

No. 0343
Arthur Zelger (1914-2004)
Tyrol, c. 1940
Innsbruck, Austria
65 x 88 cm

212

No. 0344

Ernst Keller (1891-1968)
Verpfuschter Zahn,
Verpfuschte Gesundheit,
Zahntechniker-Initiative,
Nein, 1945
Berichthaus, Zürich
128 x 90 cm

No. 0345

Niklaus Stoecklin
(1896-1982)
Bi-Oro, 1941
Wasserman, Basel
127 x 90 cm

No. 0346

Abram Games (1914-1996)
Stop=Thinking+Braking,
c. 1946
Loxley Bros. Ltd., UK
73.5 x 49 cm

No. 0347
Shepard Otis
Rails to Sales, Subway Posters, c. 1947
USA
115 x 74.5 cm

No. 0348
Erik Nitsche (1908-1998)
Say it fast . . . often . . . in color, 1947
USA
115 x 74.5 cm

No. 0349
Max Huber (1919-1992)
Gran premio dell' Autodromo, 1948
N. Moneta, Milan
139 x 97 cm

215

216

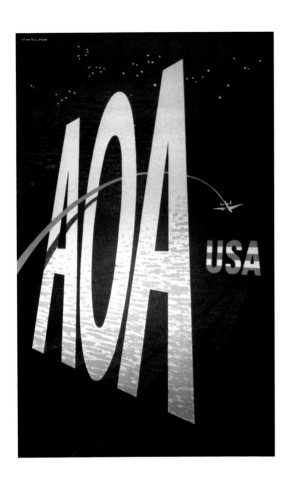

No. 0350
Heiri Steiner (1906-1983)
Schauspielhaus (poster for
a theater festival), 1946
Zurich, Switzerland

No. 0351
Lewitt-Him (Jan Lewitt,
1907-1991, and George
Him, 1900-1982)
AOA USA (American
Overseas Airlines),
c. 1946-48
UK

No. 0352
Donald Brun (1909-1999)
Bata, 1946
Switzerland

No. 0353
Erberto Carboni
(1899-1984)
50 milioni (poster for
ice cream and candy
manufacturer), 1947
Italy

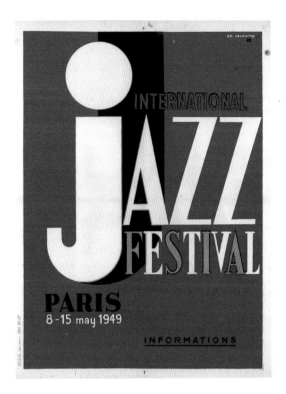

221

222

No. 0362
Guy Nouen
Algérie Pays de Lumière,
1947
Baconnier-Algeria
63.5 x 99.5 cm

No. 0363
Leo Keck (1906-1987)
Isoplastic, c. 1950
Gebr. Fretz, Zürich
21.5 x 30.5 cm

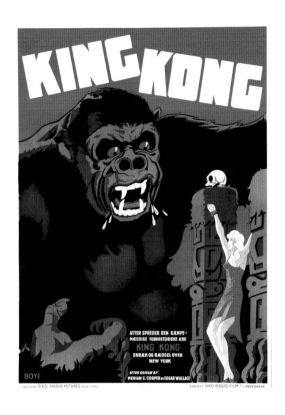

No. 0364
Alex W. Diggelmann
(1902-1987)
Zurich, 1949
J. C. Müller, Zürich
64 x 102 cm

No. 0365
Boye
King Kong (movie poster),
1948
Nornotrik
61.5 x 85 cm

No. 0366
Maggi Baaring (b. 1913)
Blenda klarer vasken
(poster for detergent),
c. 1950
Recato, Norway
71.5 x 90 cm

224

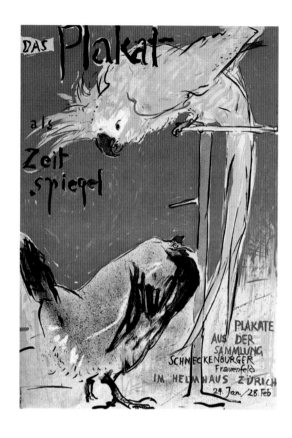

No. 0367 / No. 0368
Jean D. Macles (b. 1912)
Les frères Jacques, c. 1950
Imp. Affiches et Publicité,
Paris
40 x 60 cm

No. 0369
Hans Falk (1918-2002)
Das Plakat als Zeit Spiegel
(poster for a poster
exhibition), 1949
Zürich

No. 0370
Anders and Per Beckman
(Anders, 1907-1967, and
Per, 1913-1989)
Arbetet (poster for a
newspaper), 1950
Sweden

225

No. 0371
Stefan P. Munsing
Photo: Amann
*Ausstellung Amerikanische
Hausgeräte* (exhibition
poster), 1951
Seelig & Co., Germany
83.5 x 59 cm

No. 0372
Herbert Leupin
(1916-1999)
Pepita, 1951
Switzerland
129.5 x 89.5 cm

No. 0373
Antonio Maluf
1a Bienal, 1951
Imp. Universo, São Paulo,
Brazil
95 x 64 cm

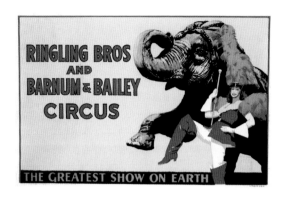

No. 0374
Artist unknown
Ringling Bros and Barnum &
Bailey Circus, 1943
USA
107 x 70.5 cm

No. 0375
Bill Bailey
Ringling Bros and Barnum &
Bailey, 1945
USA
71.5 x 52 cm

No. 0376
Bill Bailey
Ringling Bros and Barnum &
Bailey, 1945
USA
71 x 52 cm

No. 0377
Siffredi-Bardelli
San Remo, Vme Exposition
de Floriculture, 1949
N. Moneta, Milan
61.5 x 100 cm

No. 0378
Artist unknown
Holiday in Havana (movie
poster), 1949
USA
69 x 104 cm

No. 0379
Donald Brun (1909-1999)
Swissair, c. 1950
Wassermann, Basel
63.5 x100 cm

No. 0380
Am. Boh. Kraus
Ceskoslovenské Aerolinie,
c. 1945
Czechoslovakia
58.5 x 82.5 cm

230

No. 0381
Artist unknown
Plakate Fabigan (exhibition
poster), c. 1950
Austria
59 x 84 cm

No. 0382
Artist unknown
*United States International
Trade Fair*, 1950
USA
63 x 93 cm

No. 0383
Otto Baumberger
(1889-1961)
Baumann, 1952
Switzerland
91 x 129 cm

No. 0384
Charles Burki (1909-1994)
Road Lug, 1952
The Netherlands
71 x 107 cm

No. 0385
Fritz Butz (1909-1989)
Agis Pünch, 1949
Switzerland
90 x 126 cm

No. 0386
Herbert Leupin (1916-1919)
Trink Coca-Cola, 1954
Switzerland
90 x 127 cm

232

No. 0387
Artist unknown
Grand Guignol, c. 1950
Paris
40 x 60 cm

No. 0388
Michel de Alvis
Grand Guignol, c. 1950
Paris
40 x 60 cm

No. 0389
Helmut Funke (1908-1997)
ERP (poster for the
European Recovery
Program), 1950
54.5 x 75 cm

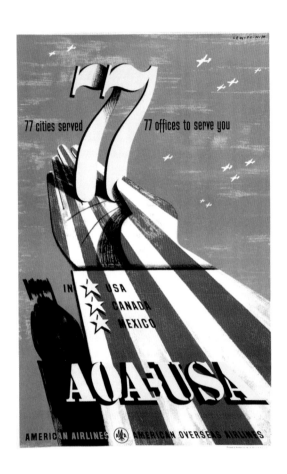

No. 0390
Lewitt-Him (Jan Lewitt,
1907-1991, and George
Him, 1900-1982)
AOA-USA, c. 1950
UK
60.5 x 95.5 cm

No. 0391
Lewitt-Him (Jan Lewitt,
1907-1991, and George
Him, 1900-1982)
AOA-USA, c. 1950
UK
60.5 x 95.5 cm

No. 0392
Artist unknown
Trông Bông Dệt Vai (poster
for cotton textiles), 1950
Vietnam
58 x 79.5 cm

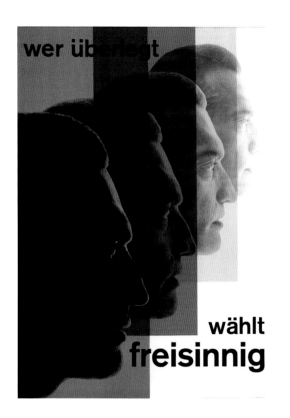

No. 0393
Achille B. Weider
*Wer überlegt wählt
freisinnig* (Vote Liberal),
c. 1950
Art. Institut Orell Füssli,
Zürich
90.5 x 128 cm

No. 0394
Croce
*Giochi Internazionali del
Mediterraneo*,1949
Arti Grafiche I.R.E.S.,
Palermo, Italy
69.5 x 100 cm

No. 0395
Edward McKnight Kauffer
(1890-1954)
American Airlines Mexico,
1948
USA
On linen, 77 x 101 cm

No. 0396
Giovanni Pintori
(1912-1998)
Olivetti Lettera 22, 1954
Ricordi, Milan
50 x 70 cm

No. 0397
H. Camy
Marchal, c. 1950
France
On linen, 23 x 32 cm

No. 0398
Raymond Savignac
(1907-2002)
Parisiennes, 1951
Offset Roto-Sadag, Geneva
127 x 89.5 cm

No. 0399
Anton Stankowsky
(1906-1998)
Perwoll, c. 1951
Germany
84.5 x 59 cm

No. 0400
Jan Wijga (1902-1978)
Philips, 1951
The Netherlands
79.5 x 60.5 cm

No. 0401
Abram Games (1914-1996)
B.O.A.C., 1950
UK
63 x 102 cm

No. 0402

Heini Fischer (b. 1921)
PKZ (poster for menswear
company), 1952
Zürich
128 x 90.5 cm

No. 0403

Joseph Binder (1898-1972)
*The most important wheels
in America*, 1952
USA

No. 0404

Walter Heinz Allner
(1909-2006)
*Cancer strikes one in five.
Strike back*, 1952
Amalgamated
Lithographers of America,
New York
115.5 x 76 cm

No. 0405

Tadeusz Trepkowski
(1914-1955)
Nie! 1952
Redakcja W.A.G. & Prasa,
Poland
99 x 69 cm

239

Überholen...?
Im Zweifel nie!

No. 0406
Josef Müller-Brockmann
(1914-1996)
*Überholen...? Im zweifel
nie!*, c. 1953
Lithographie und
Cartonnage A.G., Zürich
128 x 90 cm

THE INTERNATIONAL STYLE AND EXPRESSIONISM

European society was completely disrupted by World War II, and the period immediately following the war was a time of rebuilding cultural, social, and economic institutions. During this time, two new currents emerged. The first was a practical manifestation of Constructivism, influenced by what became known as the Swiss-inspired International Style that developed in Switzerland during the 1950s. It remained highly popular until the 1990s, and even today its influence remains evident. Basically, the International Style in graphic design is characterized by asymmetry, an underlying grid structure, "objective" photography, and flush-left, unjustified sans-serif type. Subjective design solutions were rejected in favor of a universal and systematic approach, stressing clarity and order. Pioneers of the International Style include the Swiss designers Ernst Keller and Théo Ballmer. Later, they would be joined by designers such as Max Bill, Josef Müller-Brockmann, and Armin Hofmann.

The second approach was explored by nonconformist designers who rebelled against prevailing social and artistic values. In the Netherlands this individualistic movement engendered a new expressionism in graphic design, which grew considerably during the seventies and eighties.

241

No. 0407
Josef Müller-Brockmann
(1914-1996)
Volg Traubensaft, c. 1952
A. Trüb & Cie., Switzerland
128 x 90 cm

242

243

No. 0408

Barnett Freedman
(1901-1958)
God Save Our Queen
(coronation poster), 1953
UK

No. 0409

Anders and Per Beckman
(Anders, 1907-1967, and
Per, 1913-1989)
Tag med familjen, gå på bio
(Take your family to the
movies), 1952
Sweden

No. 0410

Erberto Carboni
(1899-1984)
Bertolli, 1953
Italy

244

No. 0411

Herbert Leupin
(1916-1999)
Bale, 1952
Switzerland
63.5 x 102 cm

No. 0412

Schönhaus
Bazel, 1952
63.5 x 102 cm

No. 0413

Artist unknown
Kolynos, c. 1953
Offsetdruk de Jong & Co.,
Hilversum,
The Netherlands
119.5 x 85 cm

1 CM
IS
VOLDOENDE

KOLYNOS

DE "ZUINIGE" TANDPASTA

245

246

No. 0414

Anton Stankowsky
(1906-1998)
*Schönheit der Technik die
gute Industriform*, 1953
E. Schreiber, Stuttgart,
Germany
59.5 x 84.5 cm

No. 0415

Giovanni Pintori
(1912-1998)
Olivetti, 1953
Ind. Grafiche N. Moneta,
Italy
70 x 49.5 cm

No. 0416

L. Bernard Sargent
South Africa, c. 1953
Leiden, The Netherlands
101 x 61 cm

No. 0417

Hans Erni (b. 1909)
Impediamolo, 1954
Affiches Atar, Geneva
127 x 89 cm

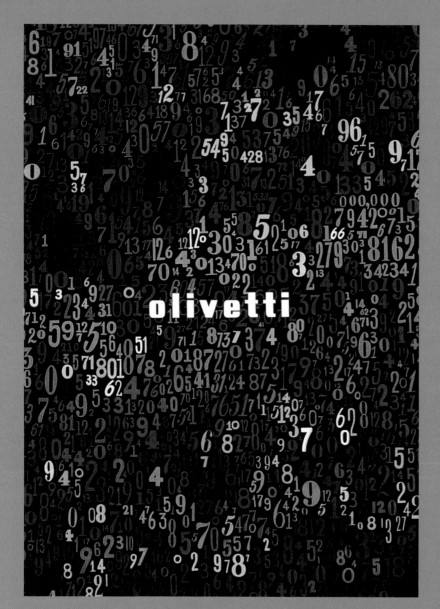

248

No. 0418
Giovanni Pintori
(1912-1998)
Olivetti, 1949
Officine Grafiche Ricordi,
Milan
70 x 49.5 cm

ITALIAN POSTWAR POSTERS

After World War II, there was a new flowering of poster design in Italy, and artists such as Armando Testa and Giovanni Pintori were among the leaders in the field. Many advances in technology were made during World War II and, when the war ended, production concentrated on consumer goods. In the 1950s, "Good design is good business" became a popular slogan for graphic designers, and insightful corporate leaders such as Adriano Olivetti recognized the value of an effective corporate image. The Olivetti Corporation, an Italian typewriter and business-machines company, was founded in 1908 by Camillo Olivetti; his son, Adriano, succeeded him as president in 1938. In 1936 Adriano employed twenty-four-year-old Giovanni Pintori to design publicity for Olivetti, a position he would hold for thirty-one years. In one of Pintori's well-known posters for Olivetti, a collage consisting only of numbers and the company logo implies the company's purpose. Pintori was especially skillful at using basic graphic shapes to symbolize the mechanical process. His abstract configurations suggest the function or purpose of the Olivetti product being advertised.

249

No. 0419

Herbert Bayer (1900-1985)
Olivetti, 1953
Italy
70 x 49.5 cm

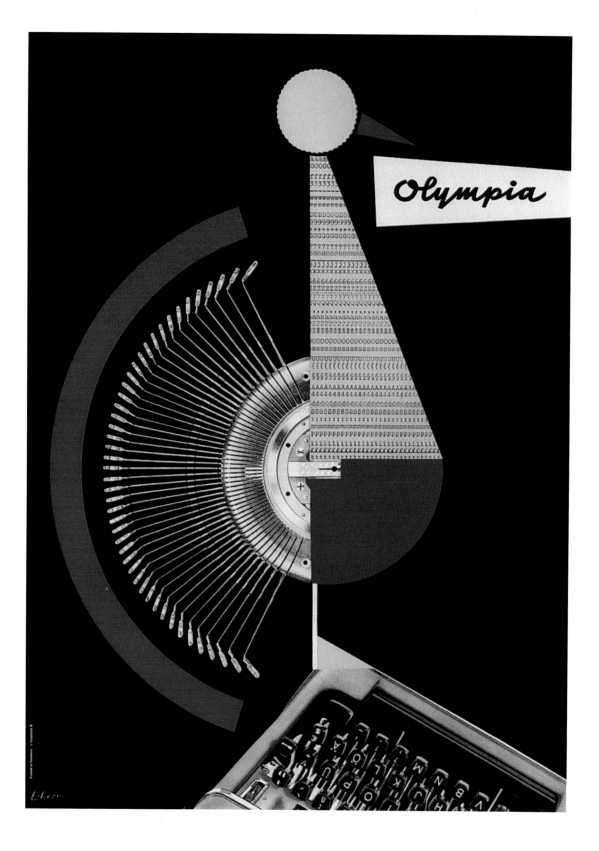

250

No. 0420
Hanns Lohrer (b. 1912)
Olympia, c. 1954
Germany
59 x 41.5 cm

No. 0421
Hanns Lohrer (b. 1912)
Olympia, c. 1954
Germany
59 x 41.5 cm

No. 0422
Hiroshi Ohchi (1908-1974)
Fuji, 1954
Japan
Silkscreen, 100 x 73 cm

No. 0423
Wim Brusse (1910-1978)
*Beelden op het
frederiksplein* (poster
for an outdoor sculpture
exhibition), 1954
The Netherlands

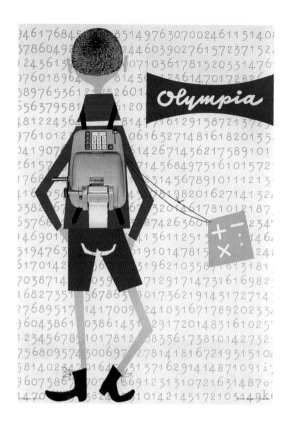

252

olympia schreibt schnell

No. 0424
Velthuys
Olympia, c. 1955
Germany
59 x 41.5 cm

No. 0425
Ofl Aicher (1922-1991)
Olympia schreibt schnell,
1954
Hochschule für Gestaltung
Ulm, Germany
59 x 41.5 cm

No. 0426
Hiroshi Ohchi (1908-1974)
Don Cossack Chorus
c. 1955
Japan
101.5 x 72.5 cm

No. 0427
Hiroshi Ohchi (1908-1974)
*Growing forms through
function* (exhibition poster),
1954
Japan
100 x 73 cm

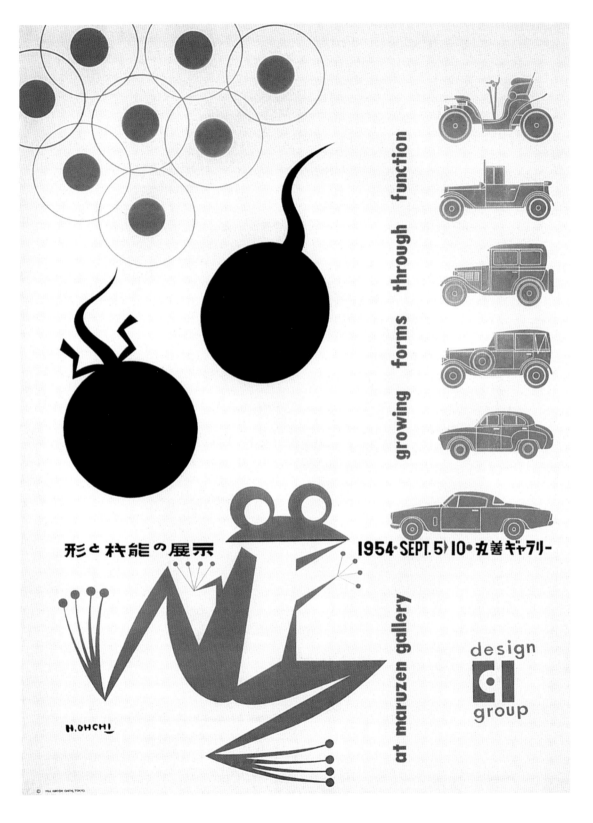

形と機能の展示

1954・SEPT. 5▷10● 丸善ギャラリー

growing forms through function

at maruzen gallery

H. OHCHI

design
di
group

254

ONE OF AME

Have yo

FORD

WHY NOT COME IN AND DO IT

REGAL PALE

CA'S 2 GREAT BEERS

...riven a

lately ?

...!

No. 0428
Artist unknown
Regal Pale, 1955
USA
42 x 93.5 cm

No. 0429
Artist unknown
Have you driven a Ford . . .
lately? 1955
USA
42 x 93.5 cm

256

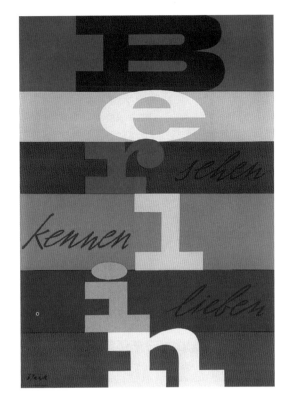

No. 0430
Yusaku Kamekura
(1915-1997)
Milliontex (textile
manufacturer), c. 1955
Dai do Keori, Japan
102 x 72.5 cm

No. 0431
Pavel Michael Engelmann
(b. 1928)
Roth-Händle, 1955
Moritz Schauenburg Lahr/
Schwarzwald, Germany
118.5 x 82.5 cm

No. 0432
Richard Blank (1901-1972)
Berlin, c. 1955
August Raabe, Berlin
84 x 60 cm

No. 0433
Otto Treumann (1919-2001)
Jaarbeurs (fair poster),
1954
Steendrukkerij de Jong &
Co., Hilversum,
The Netherlands
116 x 84 cm

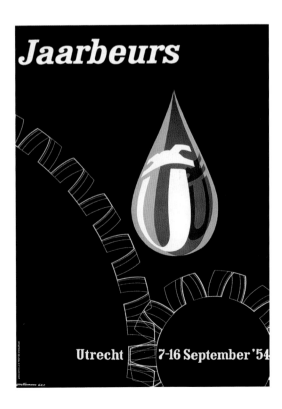

258

No. 0434
Pavel Michael Engelmann
(1928-1966)
Libella mit Schuss, 1955
Moritz Schauenburg Lahr/
Schwarzwald, Germany
118.5 x 83.5 cm

No. 0435
Abram Games (1914-1996)
*BOAC Flies to All Six
Continents*, c. 1955
UK
51 x 76 cm

No. 0436
Filo (1910-1986)
Nem, c. 1955
Offset-Nyomada-F.V.,
Hungary
97.5 x 67 cm

No. 0437
Ken Bromfield
*But nowadays . . . you can
pack parcels carefully*,
c. 1955
UK
73.5 x 92 cm

259

262

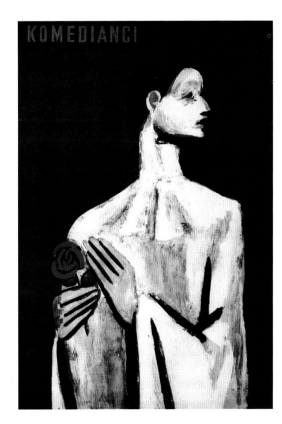

No. 0444
Pierre Boucher
(1908-2000)
*Biennale de la photographie
et du cinéma*, 1955
Paris

No. 0445
André François
(1915-2005)
DOP (shampoo), 1955
France

No. 0446
Julian Palka (1923-2002)
Komedianci (movie poster:
Les Enfants du Paradis),
1955
Poland

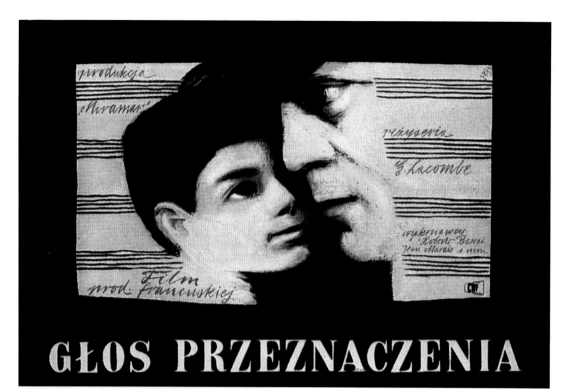

No. 0447
Julian Palka (1923-2002)
Głos Przeznaczenia (movie
poster: *L'Appel du Destin*),
1954
Poland

No. 0448
Herbert Leupin
(1916-1999)
Tribune de Lausanne, 1955
Switzerland

No. 0449
Yusaku Kamekura
(1915-1997)
Nikkor, 1955
Japan

266

MIKRON
BINOCULARS
8X50 · 7X50 · 8X35 · 6X30 · 6X18 · 6X15

NIPPON KOGAKU K.K. TOKYO JAPAN

No. 0450
Yusaku Kamekura
(1915-1997)
Mikron Binoculars, c. 1955
Nippon Kogaku, Tokyo
105.5 x 76 cm

No. 0451
Josef Mario Müller
Brockmann (1914-1996)
BEA, c. 1956
Bollmann, Zürich
127.5 x 90 cm

No. 0452
Ronald Searle (b. 1920)
Have a GOOD RUM for your money, c. 1956
R. Anderson & Co., London
75.5 x 50 cm

No. 0453
Daniele Buzzi (1890-1974)
Locarno, c. 1955
Switzerland
64 x 102 cm

No. 0454
Weber
Jungfrau Region, c. 1955
Polygraphische Gesellschaft
Laupen, Switzerland
63.5 x 102 cm

No. 0455
Herbert Leupin (1916-1999)
*Fewa . . . die sanfte
Wäsche!* (poster for
detergent), c. 1955
Switzerland
59 x 84 cm

No. 0456
Gustav G. Klutsis
(1895-1944)
*Spartakiada Moskow, For
the Unity of Worker-Class
Sportsmen All Over the
World*, 1928
USSR
105 x 150 cm

No. 0457

Cornelius van Velsen
(b. 1921)
Holland, c. 1955
De Jong & Co., Hilversum,
The Netherlands
61 x 100 cm

No. 0458

Jean George Leon Carlu
(1900-1997)
Europe, Air France, 1957
Imp. S. A. Courbet, Paris
62.5 x 100 cm

No. 0459

Arpad Elfer
Such a nice change,
Lilliput (poster for a men's
magazine), c. 1950
UK
98 x 73 cm

270

No. 0460
Herbert Leupin
(1916-1999)
Agfa, 1956
Orell Füssli, Zürich
90 x 128 cm

No. 0461
Carlo Dradi (1908-1982)
Ferrovie Nord Milano,
c. 1955
A. Mariani, Milan
70 x 100 cm

No. 0462
Mario Puppo (1905-1977)
Monte Faito, 1954
Scarpati, Casoria, Italy
70 x 100 cm

No. 0463
Bernard Villemot
(1911-1989)
Inde, Air France, 1956
On linen, 62 x 99.5 cm

No. 0464
T. Tokyo Masuda
*Japan International Trade
Fair*, 1955
Dai Nippon Printing Co.,
Japan
73 x 103 cm

No. 0465
Frans Mettes (1909-1984)
*Afrika vlieg er heen per
KLM*, 1954
The Netherlands
63.5 x 102 cm

SALAMANDER

SALAMANDER

No. 0466
Franz Weiss (1903-1982)
Salamander (poster for a
chain of stores), c. 1955
Vereinigte Kunstanstalten,
Kaufbeuren, Germany
59.5 x 84 cm

No. 0467
Franz Weiss (1903-1982)
Salamander, c. 1955
Vereinigte Kunstanstalten,
Kaufbeuren, Germany
59.5 x 84 cm

No. 0468
Artist unknown
*The Man who Loved
Redheads* (movie poster),
1955
USA
68 x 101 cm

273

No. 0469
Herbert Leupin
(1916-1999)
Ford, 1954
Switzerland
90 x 128 cm

No. 0470
Artist unknown
Bus Stop (movie poster),
1956
USA
35 x 91 cm

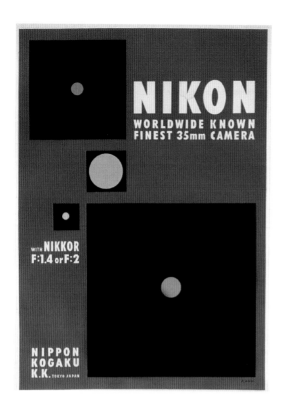

274

No. 0471
Yusaku Kamekura
(1915-1997)
Nikon, c. 1957
Japan
102 x 72 cm

No. 0472
Donald Brun (1909-1999)
Postgesetz, c. 1955
Säuberlin & Pfeiffer, Vevey,
Switzerland
91 x 128 cm

No. 0473
Leo Lionni (1910-1999)
Olivetti, c. 1956
Italy
68 x 48 cm

No. 0474
Cornelius van Velsen
(1921-2010)
Philips for Jazz, c. 1955-56
The Netherlands
74 x 54 cm

275

Liga gegen Tierquälerei und Vivisektion

Hilf den Hilflosen! Werde Mitglied der Liga gegen Tierquälerei und Vivisektion, Wien XVII., Scherlandgasse 15 - U 50746 B

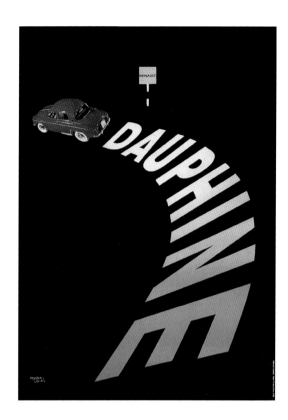

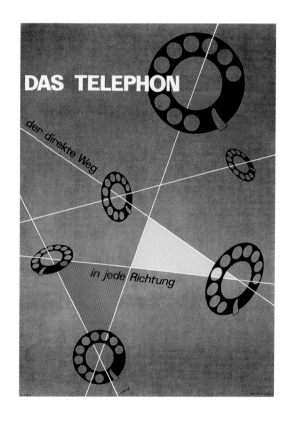

No. 0475

Hans Fabigan (1910-1975)
*Liga gegen Tierquälerei und
Vivisektion* (poster for the
prevention of cruelty to
animals), c. 1956
Piller-Druck, Vienna
119 x 84 cm

No. 0476

Herbert Leupin
(1916-1999)
Dauphine, 1957
Hug & Söhne, Zürich
127.5 x 90 cm

No. 0477

Schol
Das Telephone, 1957
Gebr. Fretz, Zürich
128 x 90 cm

278

No. 0478
Georges Calame
(1930-1999)
Le Gaz, 1958
Switzerland

No. 0480
Erberto Carboni
(1899-1984)
Barilla (poster for pasta
manufacturer), 1958
Italy

No. 0479
Jan Lenica (1928-2001)
Niebieski Ptak (movie
poster: *Il Bidone*), 1957
Poland

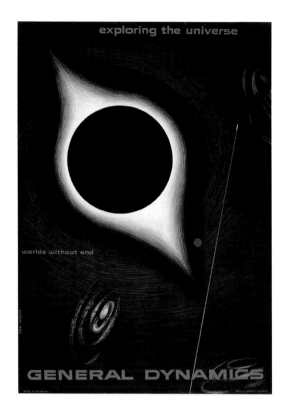

No. 0485

Nicolaas Wijnberg
(1918-2006)
Shakuntala (theater poster),
1958
Irisprint Luii & Co.,
Amsterdam
121.5 x 88.5 cm

No. 0486

Erik Nitsche (1908-1998)
General Dynamics, 1958
Lithos R. Massens,
Lausanne
120.5 x 86 cm

No. 0487

P. Pankiewicz
Hamlet, 1958
Poland
84 x 57 cm

283

284

No. 0488
Frans Mettes (1909-1984)
Sketch, Virginia Cigarettes,
c. 1960
Mouton & Co., The Hague,
The Netherlands
86 x 116 cm

No. 0489
F. Lojacono
Lambretta li, 1959
Graf. A., Milan
On linen, 98 x 68.5 cm

No. 0490
Hermann Eidenbenz
(1902-1993)
Kieler Woche (summer
festival), 1959
Germany

285

No. 0491

Red Yates
Ski Colorado, c. 1960
USA
71.5 x 107 cm

No. 0492

Donald Brun (1909-1999)
Her faithful friend, c. 1955
Joh. Roth, Munich
119.5 x 79.5 cm

No. 0493

Georges Braques
(1882-1963)
L'atelier de Braque, 1961
Mourlot, Paris
50 x 73 cm

286

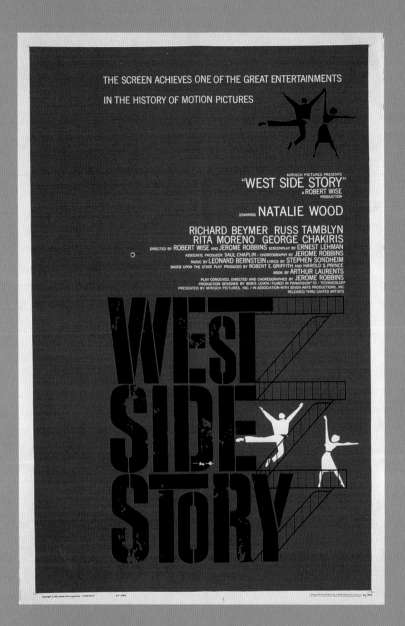

No. 0494
Saul Bass (1920-1996)
West Side Story (movie
poster), 1961
USA
104.5 x 68.5 cm

THE NEW YORK SCHOOL

Although Paris had been the center of the artistic avant-garde during the latter decades of the nineteenth century and the first half of the twentieth century, New York City assumed this role shortly before and immediately following World War II.

Having a profound understanding of European modernism, the American graphic designer Paul Rand was one of the principal forces in formulating an American approach to modern graphic design. The ideas of the New York School were imported to California by Saul Bass, when he began a design studio in Los Angeles in 1952. He often used handwriting as well as typography in his posters, especially those promoting films, and he frequently employed forms cut from paper.

Until the end of the 1950s, most display type was still was still being set by hand in the manner of Gutenberg. However, after the introduction of phototype in 1960, metal type was soon relegated mainly to independent letterpress printers. It was the American graphic designer Herb Lubalin who first exploited the creative possibilities of phototypography. Letterspacing could now be completely controlled by the designer, a much wider range of typefaces was possible, and letters could be easily expanded, condensed, or italicized. Phototypography also sharply lowered the cost of producing new typefaces. In 1965, Visual Graphics Corporation, the producer of the PhotoTypositor display typesetting machine, held a type-design competition, and Lubalin's winning designs generated quite a sensation.

287

No. 0495
Saul Bass (1920-1996)
Vertigo (movie poster),
1958
USA
104.5 x 68.5 cm

meubels AP originals

furniture meubles möbel mobili

No. 0496
Gerard Wernars (b. 1924)
Meubels AP Originals, 1959
Steendrukkerij de Jong
& Co., Hilversum, The
Netherlands
95 x 69 cm

No. 0497
Viggo Vagnby (1896-1966)
Odense Denmark, 1962
Denmark
62 x 100 cm

No. 0498
Raymond Savignac
(b. 1907)
Gitanes, 1954
Bedos & Cie, Paris
161.5 x 121 cm

No. 0499
Artist unknown
Bus Stop (movie poster),
1956
USA
58 x 83 cm

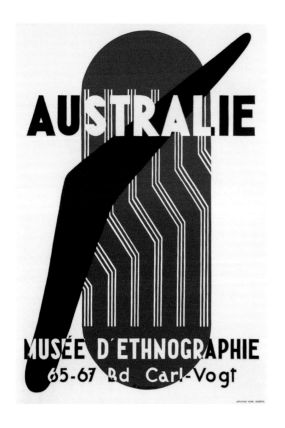

No. 0500
P. H. Chastonay
Australie, c. 1955
Atar, Geneva
65 x 94.5 cm

No. 0501
Saul Bass (1921-1996)
The Man with the Golden Arm (movie poster), 1955
USA
45 x 64.5 cm

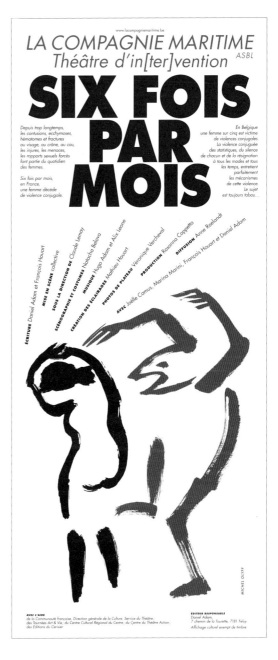

291

No. 0502

Hans Hillmann (b. 1925)
Abend der Gaukler (movie
poster: *Gycklarnas Afton*),
c. 1958
Germany
84.5 x 60.5 cm

No. 0503

Michel Olyff (b. 1927)
Six fois par mois (theater
poster), c. 1954
Belgium

No. 0504
Donald Brun (1909-1999)
Gauloises, 1959
Säuberlin & Pfeiffer, Vevey,
Switzerland
127.5 x 90 cm

No. 0505
Pierre Bonnard (1867-1947)
Bonnard Lithographies,
1957
L. Détruit-Imp. d'Art, Paris
45 x 63.5 cm

No. 0506
Riewe
Süddeutsche Zeitung,
c. 1958.
Theodor Dietz, Munich
119 x 83.5 cm

No. 0507
Charles Henri Honore
Loupot (1892-1962)
Rapha, 1959
Bedos & Cie, Paris
157 x 115 cm

293

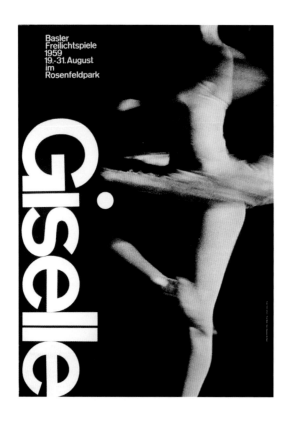

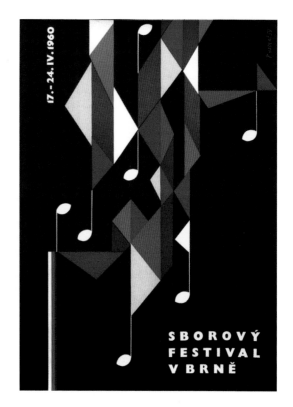

No. 0508

Armin Hofmann (b. 1920)
Giselle, 1959
Wassermann, Basel
90.5 x 128 cm

No. 0509

P. Hadlac
Sborovy Festival v Brně
(poster for a choir festival),
1959
Czechoslovakia
60 x 84 cm

MONTE-CARLO

No. 0510
Jean Gabriel Domerque
(1889-1962)
Monte-Carlo, c. 1960
Imprimerie Nationale,
Monaco
On linen, 62.5 x 100 cm

No. 0511
Edi Hauri (1911-1988)
Auto Salon, 1957
Affiches Atar, Geneva
49.5 x 64 cm

No. 0512
Jean David (1908-1993)
Visit Israel, c. 1960
Government Tourist Office
of Israel

296

No. 0513

Mario Puppo (1905-1977)
Santo Stefano d'Aveto,
vc. 1960
Sigla Effe, Geneva
On linen, 68.5 x 97.5 cm

No. 0514

Hiroshi Ohchi (1908-1974)
Japan, c. 1960
Japan Tourist Association
72.5 x 103.5 cm

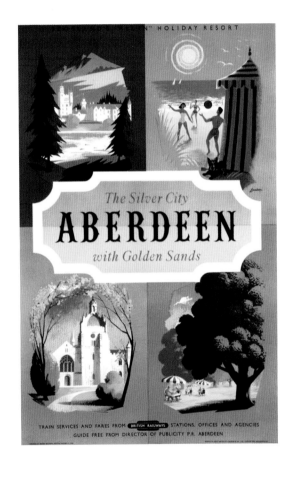

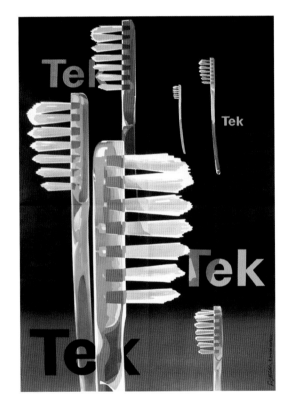

No. 0515

R. M. Lander
Aberdeen, c. 1960
Jordison & Co., London
63 x 101 cm

No. 0516

Fritz Bühler (1909-1963)
Tek, c. 1958
Switzerland

298

No. 0517
Roman Cieslewicz
(1930-1996)
Zezowate Szczescie (movie
poster), 1959
Poland
81.5 x 58.5 cm

POLISH POSTERS

Polish cities were in ruins after World War II, and one objective of the new poster culture was to bolster reconstruction. Designers such as Roman Cieslewicz, Jan Lenica, and Waldemar Swierzy increasingly used photography as a creative design medium. Symbolism and metaphor were part of the Polish poster designer's vocabulary that invited the active participation of the viewer. Unlike in the Soviet Union, avant-garde poster designers in Poland received the active support of government agencies. Among others, clients included theaters, operas, cinemas, circuses, orchestras, and tourist boards. Polish designers played a major role in determining the form of the postwar poster. Beginning in 1966, this was augmented by the International Poster Biennial held in Warsaw. Sadly, the removal of the Iron Curtain had a detrimental effect upon Polish poster design. Government support evaporated, and the influence of commercial posters from Western Europe diluted the style's intensity and originality.

Lenica enjoyed a long and productive career, creating posters that were lyrical and dramatic and often displayed overtones of Surrealism. At times he adapted Art Nouveau devices that he converted into his own style, using strong colors and vigorous lines. Swierzy's posters have often been compared to those of Milton Glaser. A skilled draftsman, Swierzy used both symbolism and caricature and is especially known for his posters depicting jazz and rock musicians. Although initially influenced by painting, Cieslewicz switched to collage and photomontage during the 1960s. He often worked on film itself and retouched photographs with ink and watercolor.

No. 0518
Jósef Mroszczak
(1910-1975)
Boris Godunov (opera poster), c. 1959
Poland

No. 0519
Wojciech Zamecznik
(b. 1923)
Pociąg (movie poster), 1959
Poland
97.5 x 130 cm

302

No. 0520

Artist unknown
Kennedy for President, 1960
USA
52.5 x 34 cm

No. 0521

Almir da Silva Mavignier
(b. 1925)
Arp (exhibition poster),
1960
Siebdruck Miller Museum
Ulm, Germany
84 x 59 cm

No. 0522

Hans Hillmann (b. 1925)
Der kleine Ausreisvser
(movie poster), c. 1960
P. R. Wilk, Germany
83.5 x 59.5 cm

304

No. 0523
Fonteray
Blanc, c. 1960
France
60 x 40 cm

No. 0524
Dick Elffers (1910-1990)
Holland Festival, 1960
Steendrukkerij de Jong
& Co., Hilversum, The
Netherlands
100 x 62 cm

No. 0525
Hans Michel (1920-1996)
and Günther Kieser
(b.1930)
Hessischer Rundfunk
(poster for radio concerts),
c. 1960
Siebdruck H. Brandt,
Frankfurt
84.5 x 118 cm

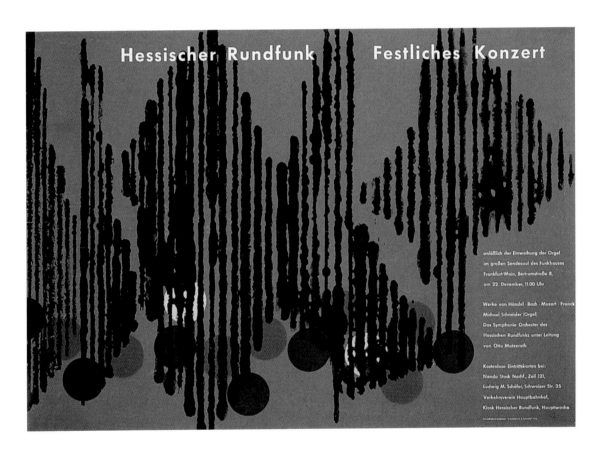

305

306

rispettate segnali e segni

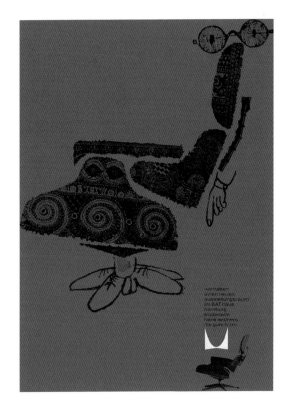

No. 0526

Abram Games (1914-1996)
Guinness, c. 1960
Mills & Rockleys Ltd.,
Ipswich, UK
76 x 50.5 cm

No. 0527

Hans Thöni (1906-1980)
Rispettate segneali e segni
(poster for traffic safety),
c. 1960
J.C. Müller, Switzerland
127.5 x 90 cm

No. 0528

Hans Michel (1920-1996)
and Günther Kieser
(b. 1930)
Poster for Eames Lounge
Chair, c. 1960
P. R. Wilk, Frankfurt
84 x 59 cm

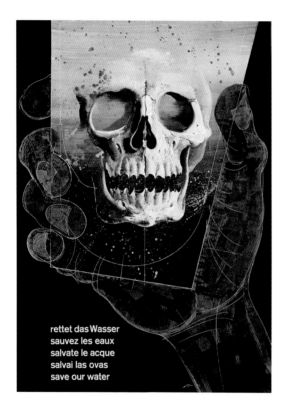

308

No. 0529

Hans Erni (b. 1909)
Rettet das Wasser, 1961
Conzett & Huber, Zürich
128 x 90.5 cm

No. 0530

Patrick Tilley
Perceptive, 1960
UK
75.5 x 50 cm

No. 0531

Werner Weissbrodt
(b. 1928)
Das Auto von morgen (The
Car of Tomorrow), 1960
L. Geissendörfer Söhne,
Karlsruhe, Germany
83.5 x 58.5 cm

das Auto von morgen

Ergebnis eines Wettbewerbs der Ford-Werke A. G. Köln

Ausstellung vom 3.-28. September 1958 in Karlsruhe Landesgewerbeamt Neubau

Karl- Friedrichstr. 17 Eingang Hebelstrasse täglich 11-13h und 15-19h Eintritt frei

Bellissima

310

Prädikat besonders wertvoll
Mit Anna Magnani und Walter Chiari
Regie: Luchino Visconti

Verleih: Neue Filmkunst Walter Kirchner

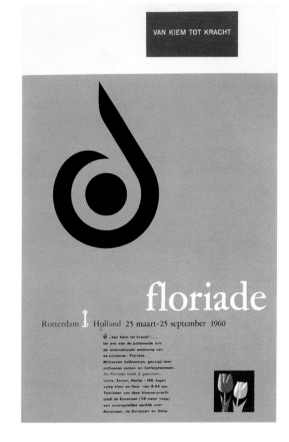

No. 0532

Hans Hillmann (b. 1925)
Bellissima (movie poster),
c. 1960
Germany
83.5 x 59.5 cm

No. 0533

Hans Michel (1920-1996)
and Günther Kieser
(b. 1930)
Der Killer von Alabama
(movie poster), c. 1960
Germany
83.5 x 59 cm

No. 0534

Kees van Roemburg
(1914-2002)
Floriade (horticultural
exhibition), 1960
The Netherlands
102 x 64 cm

312

No. 0535
Herbert W. Kapitzki
(1925-2005)
Messen und Prüfen
(exhibition poster), 1962
Germany

No. 0536
Ryuichi Yamashiro
(1920-1997)
Poster for the 2nd
International Print Biennale
in Tokyo, 1960
Japan

No. 0537
Donald Brun (1909-1999)
Tenta (awning company),
1960
Switzerland

313

MIESZKANIE NR 8

FILM PRODUKCJI JUGOSŁOWIAŃSKIEJ

REŻYSERIA: NIKOLA TANHOFER

W ROLI GŁÓWNEJ: M. ŽIVANOVIĆ

PRODUKCJA AVALA FILM

314

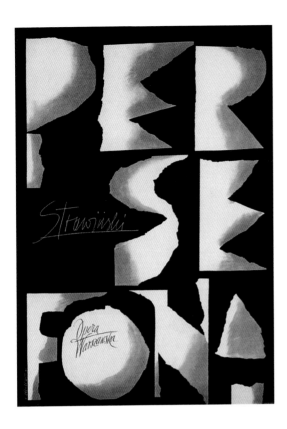

No. 0538
Roman Cieslewicz
(1930-1996)
Mieszkanie nr. 8 (movie
poster),1961
Poland
83.5 x 58.5 cm

No. 0539
Roman Cieslewicz
(1930-1996)
Persefon (opera poster),
1961
Poland
95 x 67 cm

No. 0540
Wojciech Zamecznik
(b. 1923)
S.O.S. Titanic (movie
poster), 1961
Poland
81 x 56.5 cm

318

No. 0546
T. Miyanaga
Tokyo, c. 1965
Hosokawa, Japan
72.5 x 103.5 cm

No. 0547
Harry Wysocki
JAL, c. 1965
Japan
59.5 x 79 cm

No. 0548
T. Miyanaga
Japan, Hakone National Park, c. 1960
Dai Nippon Printing Co., Japan
73 x 103 cm

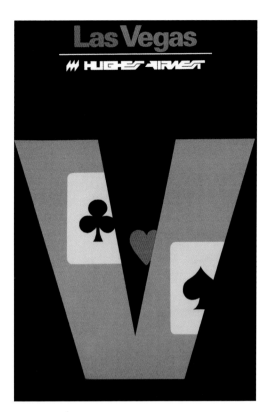

No. 0549
David Klein (1918-2005)
Africa, Fly TWA, c. 1960
USA
63.5 x 101.5 cm

No. 0550
Mario Armond
Las Vegas, c. 1960.
Zamparelli & Co., Los
Angeles
57 x 87.5 cm

No. 0551
David Klein (1918-2005)
Rome, Fly TWA Jets, c. 1960
USA
63.5 x 101.5 cm

DIE XVII OLYMPISCHEN SPIELE

ROMA   25.VIII–11.IX

320

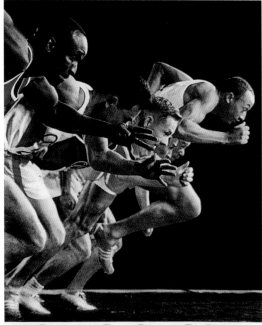

No. 0552
Armando Testa (1917-1992)
*Die XVII Olympischen Spiele
Roma*, 1960
IGAP-Milano-Roma, Italy
70 x 100 cm

No. 0553
Yusaku Kamekura
(1915-1997)
Tokyo 1964, 1964
Dai Nippon Printing Co.,
Japan
72.5 x 105.5 cm

No. 0554
Yusaku Kamekura
(1915-1997)
Tokyo 1964, 1962
Dai Nippon Printing Co.,
Japan
104 x 72.5 cm

No. 0555
Dorothea (b. 1921) and
Fritz Fischer-Nosbisch
(b. 1919)
Das verflixte 7. Jahr (movie
poster), c. 1965
59 x 84 cm

No. 0556
G. van den Eynde
To Belgium by Sabena,
c. 1960
Linsmô, Brussels
64.5 x 100 cm

No. 0557
Yrani
Norway Viking Wonderland,
1962
Trygve B. Perdersen &
Sønn, Oslo
62.5 x 100 cm

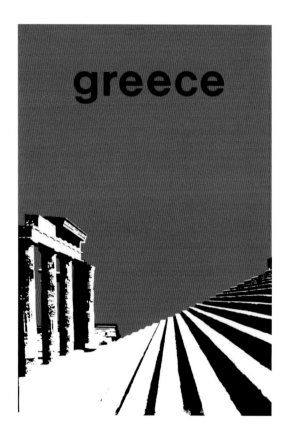

322

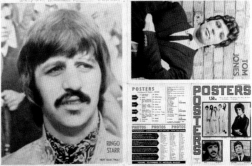

No. 0560 / No. 0561
Artist unknown
Posters, c. 1967
USA
Front and back,
89 x 112.5 cm

No. 0562

Hans Hillmann (b. 1925)
Sturn über Asien (movie
poster), 1961
Silkscreen novum,
Germany
84 x 61 cm

No. 0563

Benno Wissing (b. 1923)
Plannenmaken (exhibition
poster), 1961
Steendrukkerij de Jong
& Co., Hilversum, The
Netherlands
105 x 74.5 cm

No. 0564

Manfred Bingler (b. 1928)
Swissair, 1961
Imago, Zürich
102 x 64 cm

326

No. 0565

E. Erich Strenger
*European Hillclimb
Championship*, 1961
Autenrieth, Stuttgart,
Germany
118.7 x 84.4 cm

No. 0566

Zofia Stryjeriska
(1894-1976)
Rudy (movie poster), 1961
58 x 84 cm

No. 0567

Günther Rambow (b. 1938)
and Gerhard Lienemeyer
(b. 1936)
Gold Rausch (movie
poster), 1962
Obpacher, Munich
85 x 59 cm

No. 0568

Lajos Görög
Avád Tanuja (movie
poster: *Witness for the
Prosecution*), 1961
Hungary
80.5 x 56.5 cm

MAGYARUL BESZÉLŐ AMERIKAI FILM*

GYÁRTÓ ÉS FORGALMAZÓ:

UNITED ARTISTS

*MARLENE DIETRICH,
TYRONE POWER
ÉS CHARLES LAUGHTON
FŐSZEREPLÉSÉVEL

A VÁD TANUJA

NEM AJÁNLOTT

14 ÉVEN ALUL

No. 0573
Celestino Piatti (b. 1922)
Photo: Siegfried
Bell, 1962
VSK, Basel
127.5 x 90 cm

No. 0574
Hubert Hilscher (b. 1924)
Fly by Lot, 1962
RSW Prasa, Katowice,
Poland
96.5 x 67 cm

No. 0575
Waldemar Swierzy
(b. 1931)
Alfred Hitchcock (poster for
a film festival), c. 1965
Poland

No. 0576
Artist unknown
Time, c. 1962
USA
111.5 x 71 cm

No. 0577
Waldemar Swierzy
(b. 1931)
Psy Wojny (movie poster:
The Dogs of War), 1981
Poland

332

FRANK
LLOYD
WRIGHT
WYSTAWA ARCHITEKTURY

WYSTAWA CZYNNA OD 5-III DO 22-III-1962
W SALACH S.A.R.P. UL. FOKSAL 2.

No. 0578
Waldemar Swierzy
(b. 1931)
Frank Lloyd Wright, 1962
Poland
97 x 67.5 cm

No. 0579
Armin Hofmann (b. 1920)
Tell (opera poster), 1963
Switzerland
128 x 90.5 cm

No. 0580
F.K.
8és1/2 (movie poster),
c. 1963
Bors Ferenc Offset
Nyomda, Budapest
81.5 x 56.5 cm

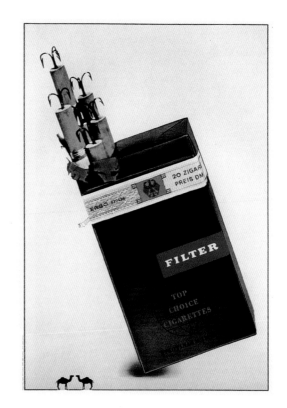

334

No. 0581

Roman Cieslewicz
(1930-1996)
Jezioro Łabedzie (ballet
poster: *Swan Lake*), 1964
Poland
97.5 x 67.5 cm

No. 0582

Schleissing Gruppe 4
Der Hund von Baskerville
(movie poster), 1964
Germany
58 x 82.5 cm

No. 0583

Klaus Staeck (b. 1938)
Camel, c. 1963
Steidl, Göttingen, Germany
84 x 59.5 cm

No. 0584

Roman Cieslewicz
(1930-1996)
Zawrot Głowy (movie
poster: *Vertigo*), 1963
Poland
83 x 59 cm

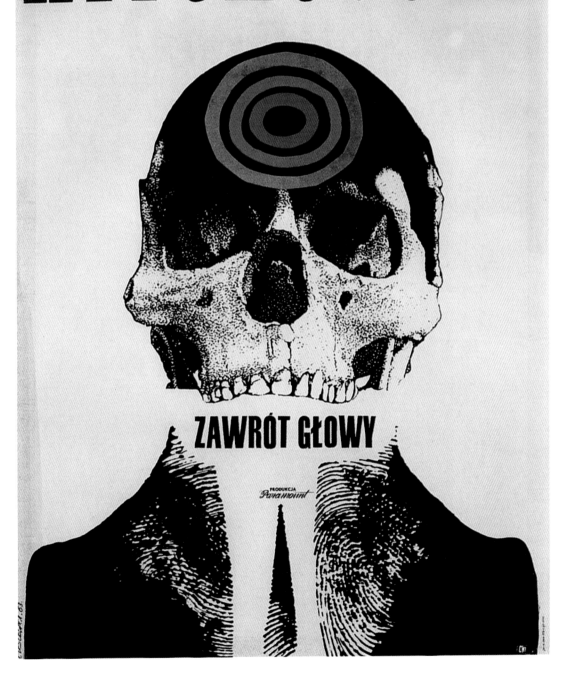

KIM NOVAK W PODWÓJNEJ ROLI | JAMES STEWART
BARBARA DEL GEDDES W MROŻĄCYM KREW W ŻYŁACH 🖝 BARWNYM FILMIE

HITCHCOCKA

ZAWRÓT GŁOWY

PRODUKCJA
Paramount

335

LINGE
ENCORE
PLUS
PROPRE

337

No. 0585
Raymond Savignac
(b. 1907)
Omo (laundry detergent),
1963
Synergie-Edit., Paris
157 x 115 cm

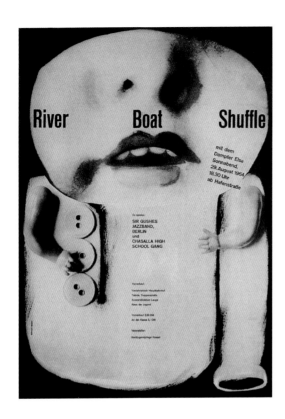

No. 0586
Jan Lenica (1928-2001)
Alban Berg, Wozzeck, 1964
Poland
94 x 66.5 cm

No. 0587
Hans-Jürgen Spohn
(b. 1934)
River Boat Shuffle, c. 1964
Germany
83.5 x 59 cm

No. 0588
Jan Lenica (1928-2001)
Nóz w Wodzie (movie poster:
Knife in the Water), 1964
Poland

340

No. 0589
Roman Cieslewicz
(1930-1996)
Raj Utracony (opera poster:
Paradise Lost), 1980
Poland

No. 0590
Henry Wolf (1925-2005)
Gino Severini, 1963
Museum Boijmans van
Beuningen, Rotterdam,
The Netherlands

No. 0591
Hans Falk (1918-2002)
*Zu Land und zu Wasser ein
Spiegel der Heimat sein*
(exhibition poster), 1964
Lausanne

No. 0592
Jósef Mroszczak
(1910-1975)
Verdi, Don Carlos, 1963
Poland

341

342

343

No. 0593
Tomi Ungerer (b. 1931)
Dr. Strangelove (movie
poster), 1964
USA

No. 0594
Pablo Palazuelo (b. 1916)
Palazuelo, c. 1965
Mourlot Imp., France
43.5 x 68 cm

No. 0595
Hans-Jürgen Spohn
(b. 1934)
Blue Note, c. 1965
Germany
83 x 59 cm

No. 0596
J. Treutler
*XX Międzynarodowe
Zawody Narciarskie*, 1965
68 x 98 cm

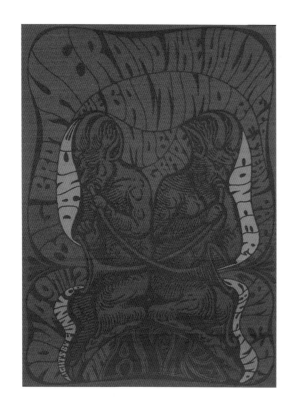

344

WORLD HEAVYWEIGHT CHAMPIONSHIP
SEPTEMBER 28, 1976
YANKEE STADIUM
NEW YORK CITY

MUHAMMAD ALI • KEN NORTON

Top Rank, Inc. Madison Square Garden

No. 0599

Armand Perrenet
*The First Holiness
Kitschgarden for the
Liberation of Love and
Peace in Colours* (rock
festival), 1968
The Netherlands
43 x 61 cm

No. 0600

Michael English (b. 1941)
UFO Coming, 1967
Osiris Visions Ltd., London
50 x 74.5 cm

No. 0601

Luigi Castiglioni
*Muhammad Ali – Ken
Norton*, 1976
USA
On linen, 40.5 x 52 cm

No. 0602
David Klein (1918-2005)
Spain Fly TWA, c. 1965
USA
63.5 x 102 cm

No. 0604
David Klein (1918-2005)
Europe Fly TWA, c. 1965
USA
63.5 x 102 cm

No. 0603
David Klein (1918-2005)
Holy Land Fly TWA Jets,
c. 1965
USA
63.5 x 102 cm

No. 0605
Be Verdier
New Orleans, c. 1965
58.5 x 89 cm

No. 0606
Artist unknown
Las Vegas Western Airlines,
c. 1965
USA
63 x 98.5 cm

No. 0607
Atelier Ade
Zoo Wuppertal, c. 1965
Germany
60 x 84 cm

No. 0608
Dan Reisinger (b. 1934)
ELAL Copenhagen, c. 1965
49 x 69 cm

No. 0609
Josef Müller-Brockmann
(b. 1914)
Giuseppe Verdi, Requiem,
1967
Bollmann, Zürich
70x100

No. 0610
Strom
Fasching in München, 1967
Klein & Volbert, Munich
59 x 84 cm

No. 0611

Artist unknown

CSSR Budme Pevni!

(Czechoslovakia – Let's Fix

It!), 1968

Czechoslovakia

55 x 78 cm

No. 0612

Josef Müller-Brockmann

(b. 1914)

Brahms, Ein deutsches

Requiem, 1968

Bollmann, Zürich

70 x 100 cm

No. 0613

Artist unknown

1945 1968, 1968

Czechoslovakia

80.5 x 45.5 cm

350

No. 0614

Armin Hofmann (b. 1920)
Stadttheater Basel, 1966
Wassermann, Basel
90.5 x 128 cm

No. 0615

Herbert Bayer (1900-1985)
Bauhaus (exhibition
poster), 1968
Staatsgalerie Stuttgart,
Germany
59.5 x 84 cm

No. 0616

Richard Avedon
(1923-2004)
*Who Has a Better Right to
Oppose the War?*, 1969
USA
61 x 96 cm

351

No. 0617
Artist unknown
Bresil en Lutte Solidarite,
1968
50 x 75 cm

No. 0618
Atelier Populaire
SS, 1968
Paris
43 x 62 cm

No. 0619
Atelier Populaire
Oui: usines occupees, 1968
Paris
43 x 62 cm

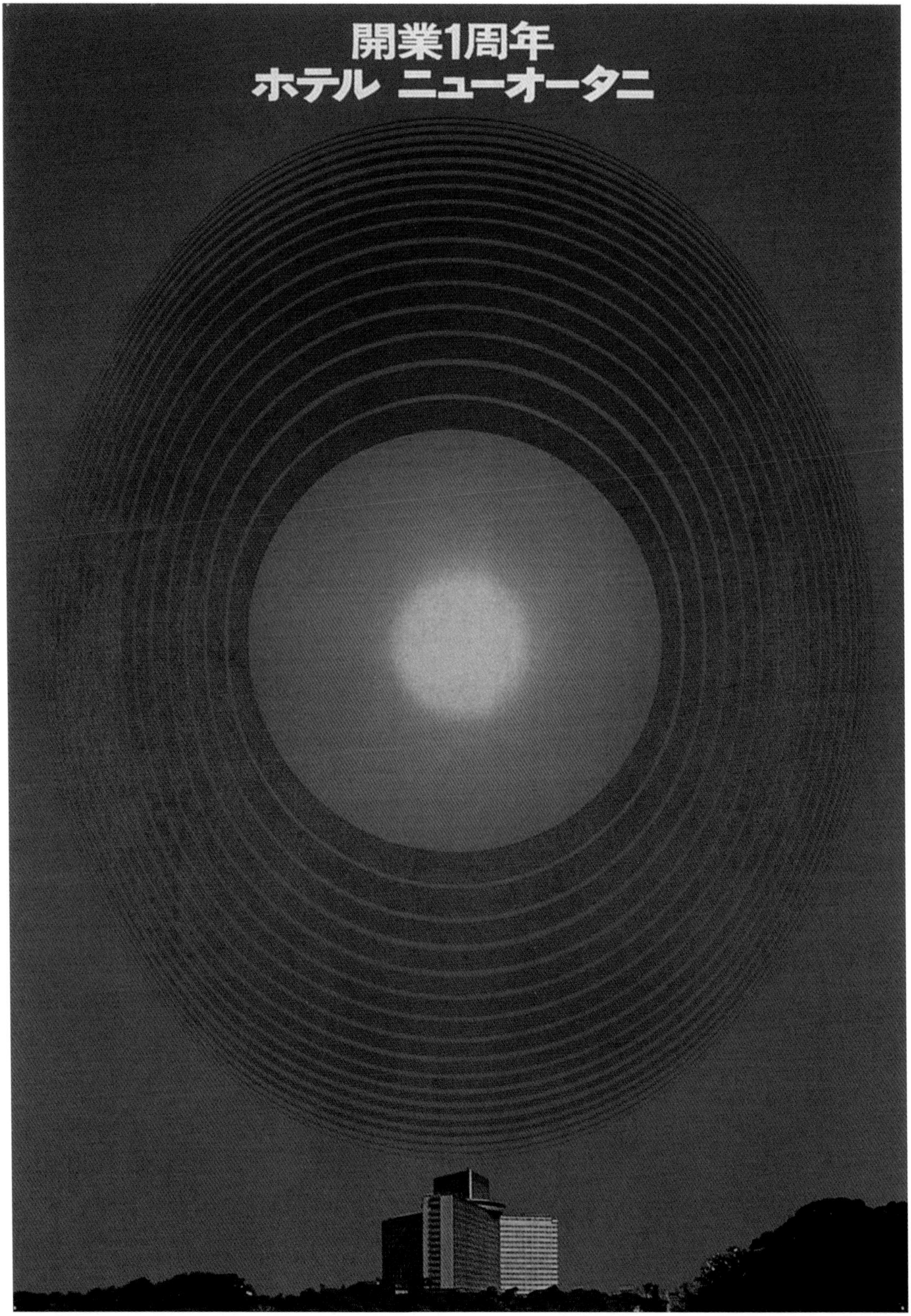

開業1周年
ホテル ニューオータニ

352

You don't have to be Jewish

to love Levy's
real Jewish Rye

No. 0620

Kazumasa Nagai (b. 1929)
New Otani Hotel, Tokyo:
First Anniversary, 1965
Japan
103 x 73 cm

No. 0621

Alton Kelley (1940-2008)
Vanilla Fudge, 1967
USA
35 x 51 cm

No. 0622

Sonja
Week-end (movie poster).
1967
Imp. Marquet., France
59 x 39 cm

No. 0623

William Taubin (b. 1916)
Photo: Howard Zieff
(1967-2009)
You don't have to be Jewish
to love Levy's
USA
114.5 x 75 cm

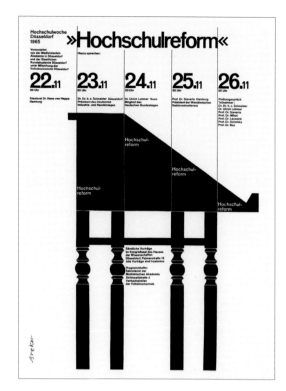

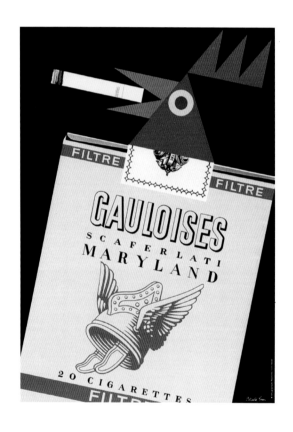

No. 0624
Donald Brun (1909-1999)
Gauloises, 1966
Paris

No. 0625
Walter Breker (1904-1980)
Hochschulreform (poster
for a lecture series on
educational reform), 1965
Düsseldorf

No. 0626
Arne Ungermann
(1902-1981)
Narkomaner (movie poster:
The Connection), 1965
Danish Museum of Art &
Design, Copenhagen

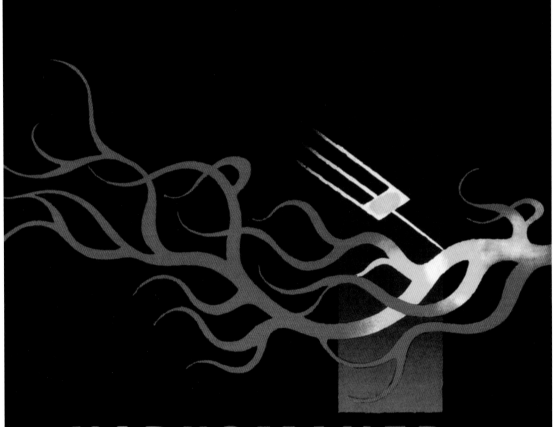

355

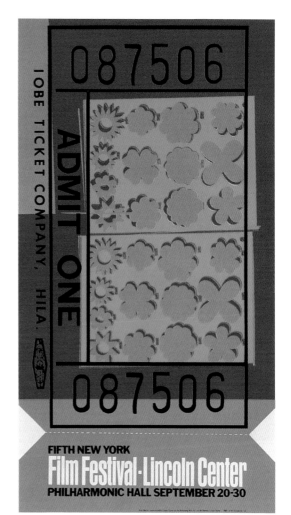

No. 0631
Martin Sharp (b. 1942)
Mister Tambourine Man,
1967
UK
76 x 51 cm

No. 0632
Alton Kelley (1940-2008)
Jefferson Airplane, 1967
USA
35.5 x 50.5 cm

No. 0633
Andy Warhol (1930-1987)
Film Festival, 1967
USA
114.5 x 61 cm

No. 0634
Pedro Ramírez Vazquez,
Eduardo Terrazas, and
Lance Wyman
Mexico 68, 1967
Impresos Automaticos de
Mexico
90 x 90 cm

359

360

No. 0635
Victor Moscoso (b. 1936)
The Chambers Bros., 1967
USA
56 x 35.5 cm

STUDENTS IN REVOLT AND POP CULTURE

Before the predominance of films and television, posters were among the most important means of visual communication. With the advent of the new media, poster production suffered a dramatic decline. However, beginning in the 1960s, popular music and the Vietnam War helped to create a resurgence of American posters by designers such as Milton Glaser, Victor Moscoso, and Peter Max. Labeled by the media as "psychedelic posters," they celebrated the antiestablishment subculture of that period. When the poster craze reached its height in the early 1970s, imaginative American poster art was often found on university campuses, one of the last remaining pedestrian milieus in the United States. Since many diverse events regularly take place at universities, the campus provides a perfect setting for the display of posters.

During the student revolts of May 1968, Parisian streets were overflowing with posters and placards, mainly designed by amateurs. Three young graphic designers, Pierre Bernard, François Miehe, and Gerard Paris-Clavel, were heavily involved with activist politics at that time. Bernard and Paris-Clavel had studied in Poland under Henryk Tomaszewski, who encouraged an intellectual approach to design combined with an unambiguous commitment to social principles. In 1970 Bernard, Miehe, and Paris-Clavel decided to form the Grapus studio to use graphic design for political, social, and cultural objectives. French left-wing radicals were then referred to as "crapules staliniennes" (Stalinist scum), and this appellation was combined with the word "graphic" to create the studio's name.

Grapus projects were always team efforts, and after thorough analysis and extensive dialogue the essence of the assignment's message was resolved. Only then would a graphic solution be sought. Grapus preferred to use universal signs with easily comprehended connotations. These included symbols such as the moon, hands, wings, flags, fireworks, and blood. Handwritten titles and graffitilike texts imbued their posters with a forceful graphic energy.

A 1982 poster promoting an exhibition of their own graphics shows a head holding in its mouth a three-dimensional arrow with cutout letters spelling the word "EXPO." Mounted on a coiled spring, it has Mickey Mouse ears and the hair and mustache of Hitler; its eyes consist of the French tricolor and the Communist hammer and sickle. The Grapus style was widely emulated, and the vigorous casualness of its design and graffiti-inspired lettering was soon evident in trendy advertising.

No. 0636

Michael English
(1939-2007) and Nigel
Weymouth (b. 1941)
Pink Floyd, c. 1967
UK
75.5 x 50 cm

They are agitated
by the drum
the four Bacabs ride
on the back of a green
rainbow
beneath on
as beyond the stars fall

362

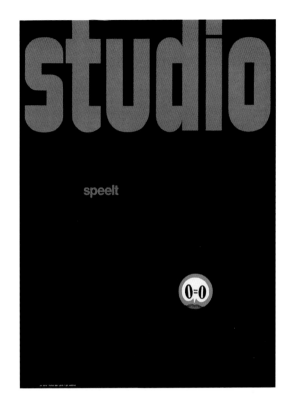

No. 0637
Michael English
(1939-2007) and Nigel
Weymouth (b. 1941)
*Crazy World of Arthur
Brown*, c. 1967
Osiris Vision Ltd., UK
75 x 50 cm

No. 0638
Michael English
(1939-2007) and Nigel
Weymouth (b. 1941)
UFO Coming, 1967
UK
75 x 50 cm

No. 0639
Jan Bons (b. 1918)
Studio, 1969
The Netherlands
115.5 x 82.5 cm

No. 0640
Peter Max (b. 1937)
Toulouse Lautrec, 1967
USA
91.5 x 61 cm

364

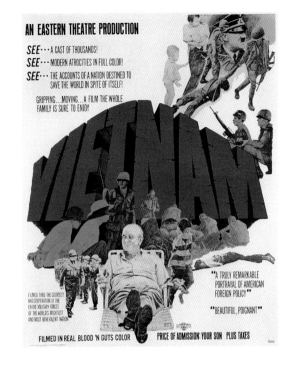

No. 0641
Artist unknown
Rosemary's Baby, 1968
Paramount, USA
84.5 x 62 cm

No. 0642
J. Michaelson
Nixon's the One!, 1968
LPIU, St. Louis, USA
56 x 35.5 cm

No. 0643
Nordahl
Vietnam (movie poster),
1968
Gross National Product, USA
72.5 x 58 cm

No. 0644
Bonnie MacLean. (b. 1961)
Blue Cheer, 1967
USA
35.5 x 53.5 cm

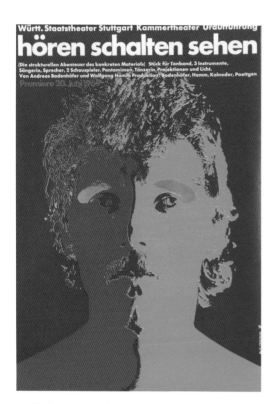

366

No. 0645
F. & R. Grindler
Hören Schalten Sehen
(theater poster), 1969
Fauss-Siebdruck
58.5 x 86 cm

No. 0646
Roman Cieslewicz
(1930-1996)
CCCP USA, 1968
Poland
54.5 x 81.5 cm

No. 0647
Wim Crouwel (b. 1928)
Vormgevers (design
exhibition), 1968
The Netherlands
63.5 x 95 cm

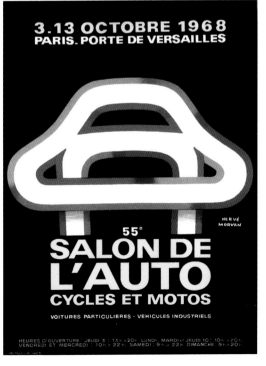

Georges Mathieu
(b. 1921)
Greece Air France, 1968
Draeger Frères, Paris
60 x 100 cm

No. 0649
Frank Stella (b. 1936)
Lincoln Centert Festival, 1967
USA
75 x 114 cm

No. 0650
Hervé Morvan (1917-1980)
Salon d'Auto (automobile
exhibition), 1968
Bedos & Cie. Imp., Paris
38.5 x 52 cm

368

No. 0651
Axelbuham Gruppe
Alaskafüchse (movie
poster), 1964
East Germany
58 x 82.5 cm

No. 0652
Milton Glaser (b. 1929)
Dylan, 1966
USA
56 x 83.5 cm

No. 0653
Artist unknown
Love, 1967
45 x 76 cm

No. 0654
Martin Sharp (b. 1942)
Vincent, 1968
London
49 x 73.5 cm

370

PAS DE RECTANGLE BLANC
POUR UN PEUPLE ADULTE:

INDÉPENDANCE et AUTONOMIE de l'O.R.T.F.

No. 0655

Atelier Populaire
Sera-t-il chomeur? (Will he
be unemployed?), 1968
France
50 x 67 cm

No. 0656

Jean Effel (1908-1982)
*Pas de rectangle blanc pour
un peuple adulte* (No white
rectangle for adult people),
1968
France
60 x 79.5 cm

372

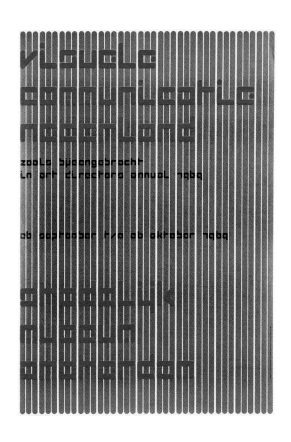

No. 0657

Roger Excoffon
(1910-1983)
Grenoble 1968, 1968
France

No. 0658

Wim Crouwel (b. 1928)
*Visuele Communicatie
Nederland*, 1969
Steendrukkerij de Jong
& Co., Hilversum, The
Netherlands
95 x 65 cm

No. 0659

Yoshio Hayakawa (b. 1917)
The Face, 1968
Japan

No. 0660

Hiromu Hara (1903-1986)
Dada (exhibition poster),
1968
Japan

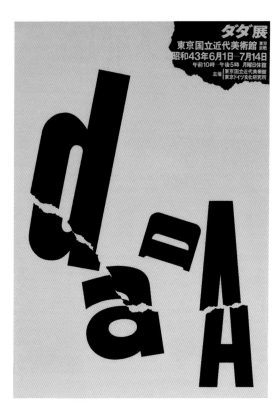

Spanje. Alles onder de zon.

Auvergne
FRENCH NATIONAL RAILROADS

No. 0661

Juan Miró (1893-1983)
España, c. 1980
Spain
185 x 126 cm

No. 0662

Salvador Dalí (1904-1989)
Auvergne, 1969
Draeger Imp., France
98 x 63 cm

No. 0663

Artist unknown
Movie poster: *Teorema*,
1969
Japan
147 x 51 cm

テオレマ

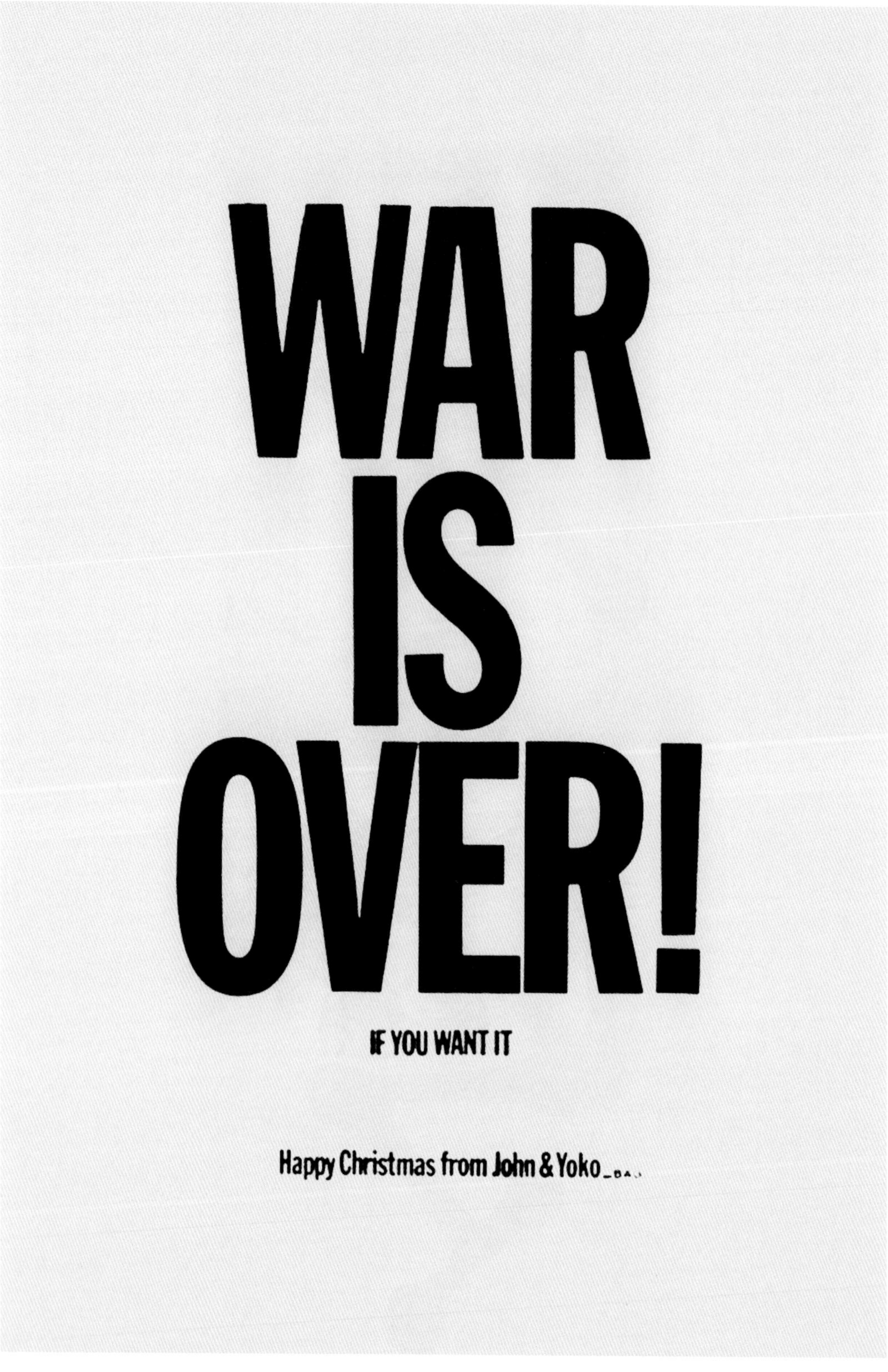

WAR IS OVER!

IF YOU WANT IT

Happy Christmas from John & Yoko ____

No. 0664
John Lennon (1940-1980)
and Yoko Ono (b. 1933)
War is Over!, 1969
The Netherlands
117.5 x 83 cm

No. 0665
Jodto Lieverst Todio
Boycott McDonalds,
c. 1969
Austria
65 x 50 cm

No. 0666
Herb Lubalin (1918-1981)
No More War!
(announcement for *Avant
Garde* magazine's antiwar
poster contest), 1968
100 x 70 cm

No. 0667
Tomi Ungerer (b. 1931)
Black Power, White Power,
c. 1970
54.5 x 71.5 cm

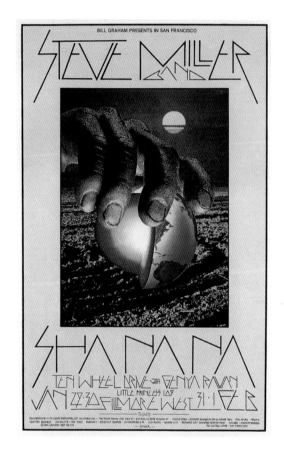

No. 0668

David Singer (b. 1941)
Steve Miller, 1970
Tea Lautrec, San Francisco
55.5 x 35.5 cm

No. 0669

Artist unknown
Berlin, c. 1970
Carl Kühn & Söhne,
Germany
84 x 59.5 cm

No. 0670

Dea Trier Morch (Denmark)
*Nødvendigheden af at
skaffe stadig øget afsætning
af produkterne jager
bourgeosiet ud over hele
jordkloden* (anticapitalist
poster), 1969
Denmark
84.5 x 60 cm

ØGET AFSÆTNING AF PRODUKTERNE JAGER BOURGEOISIET UD OVER HELE JORDKLODEN NØDVENDIGHEDEN AF AT SKAFFE STADIG

379

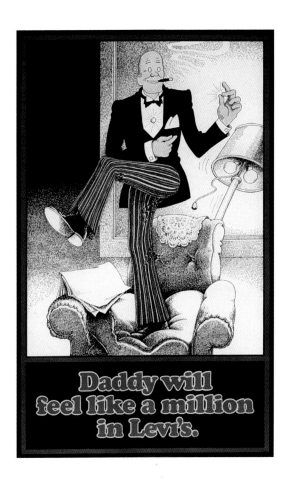

No. 0671

Peter Brandt (Artists and
Writers Protest Group)
Photo: R. L. Haeberle
Four more years? 1969
Amalgamated Lithographers,
New York
63.5 x 96.5 cm

No. 0672

Artist unknown
*Daddy will feel like a million
in Levi's,* c. 1970
USA
92 x 56.5 cm

No. 0673

George Noordanus
(b. 1944)
PSP (poster for the Pacifist
Socialist Party), 1971
The Netherlands
64 x 45 cm

No. 0674

Ryuichi Yamashiro
(1920-1997)
Seibu (department store),
1969
Japan

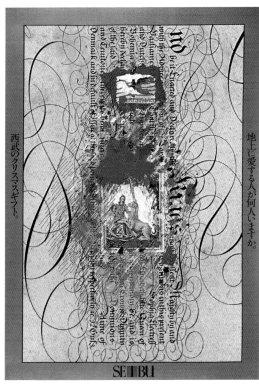

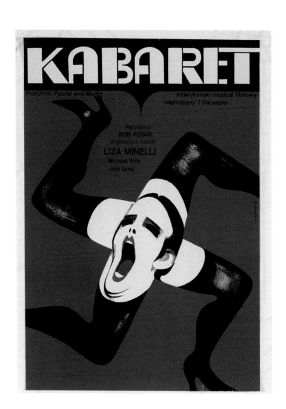

382

No. 0675

Wiktor Górka (b. 1922)
Kabaret, 1973
Poland
83.5 x 57.5 cm

No. 0676

Bernard Villemot
(1911-1989)
Perrier, c. 1970
France
45.5 x 60 cm

No. 0677

David Singer (b. 1941)
The Rolling Stones, 1972
Tea Lautrec, San Francisco
70.5 x 55.5 cm

No. 0678

Artist unknown
*Asser de morts aux
Vietnam*, 1970
France
65 x 50.5 cm

383

384

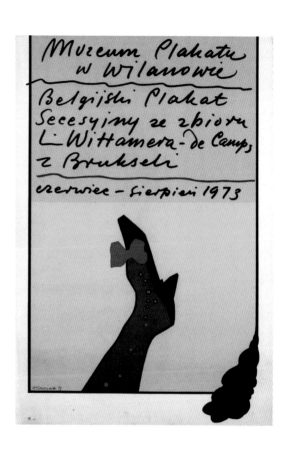

No. 0679

Dorzopykob
CPSU–Fighting Force of the World Communist Movement, 1972
Russia
59 x 87.5 cm

No. 0680

P. Hugentobler
Montana Vermala, c. 1970
Switzerland
45 x 64 cm

No. 0681

Henryk Tomaszewski
(b. 1914)
Belgijski Plakat (poster for a poster exhibition), 1973
Poland
On linen, 69.5 x 99 cm

No. 0682

Gielijn Escher (b. 1945)
Affiches, 1972
The Netherlands
52.5 x 83.5 cm

No. 0683

Josse Goffin (b. 1938)
Citroën, 1975
France
60 x 80 cm

No. 0684

Josse Goffin (b. 1938)
Citroën, 1975
France
60 x 80 cm

386

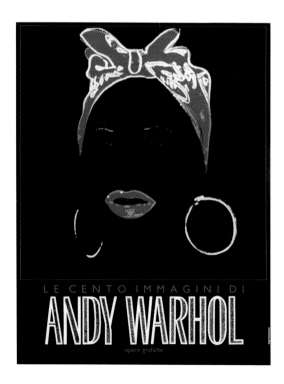

No. 0685
Bill Gold (b. 1921)
Magnum Force (movie
poster), 1973
USA
50 x 71 cm

No. 0687
Artist unknown
Straw Dogs (movie poster),
1971
USA
69 x 104 cm

No. 0686
Evelina Laviano
*Le Cento Immagini di Andy
Warhol* (exhibition poster),
1989
Museo d'Arte Contemporanea
Villa Croce, Genoa
68 x 88.5 cm

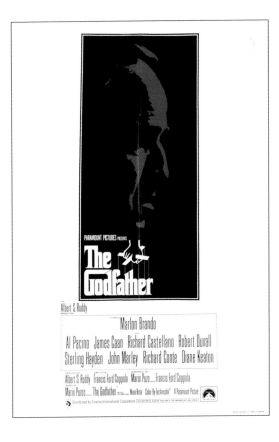

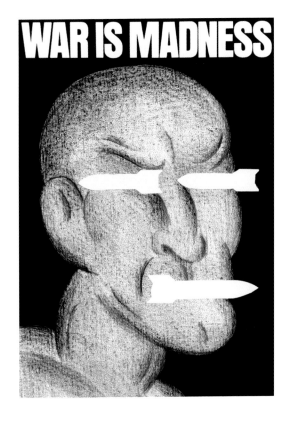

No. 0688
Artist unknown
The Godfather (movie
poster), c. 1972
USA
68 x 101.5 cm

No. 0689
Artist unknown
*The Mothers of Invention–
Absolutely Free*, 1970
USA
46 x 62 cm

No. 0690
Seymour Chwast (b.1931)
War Is Madness, 1986
USA

388

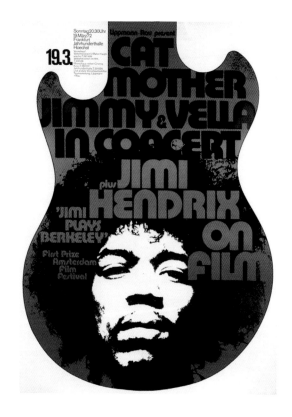

No. 0691
Silvio Coppola (1920-1985)
Poster for a restaurant,
1975
Italy

No. 0692
Günther Kieser (b. 1930)
*Procol Harum & Heads,
Hands & Feet*, 1971
Germany
60 x 84 cm

No. 0693
Günther Kieser (b. 1930)
*Cat Mother Jimmy & Vella
In Concert plus Jimi Hendrix
on Film*, 1972
Germany
60 x 85 cm

389

No. 0694
Elzbieta Procka (b. 1947)
w filmie Podroz (movie
poster: *Il Viaggio*), 1976
Poland
58 x 82 cm

No. 0695
Artist unknown
Marc Chagall Ilustrace
(exhibition poster)
The Museum of Czech
Literature (PNP), Prague

390

PEACE IS PATRIOTIC

1973

No. 0696

Student Workshop Berkeley
Peace Is Patriotic, 1973
Berkeley, California
56 x 33 cm

No. 0697

Helmut Andreas Peter
Grieshaber (1909-1981)
Chile? 1973
Germany
Woodcut, 77 x 56 cm

No. 0698

Gielijn Escher (b. 1945)
Shaffy Theater, 1974
Steendrukkerij de Jong
& Co., Hilversum, The
Netherlands
117.5 x 83 cm

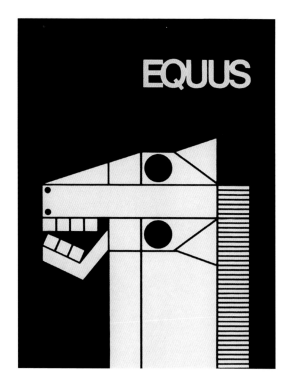

392

No. 0699
Klaus Staeck (b. 1938)
Und der Haifisch der hat Zähne (And the shark has teeth), 1975
Steidl, Göttingen, Germany
83.5 x 59 cm

No. 0700
Gilbert Lesser (b. 1935)
Equus (theater poster), 1974
USA
101 x 76 cm

No. 0701
Ida van Bladel (b. 1931)
Levi's, 1971
The Netherlands
94 x 63.5 cm

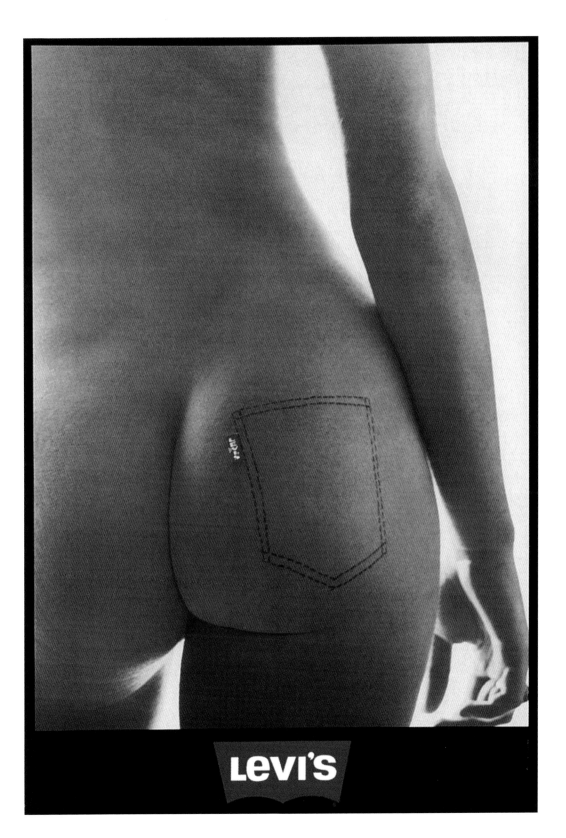

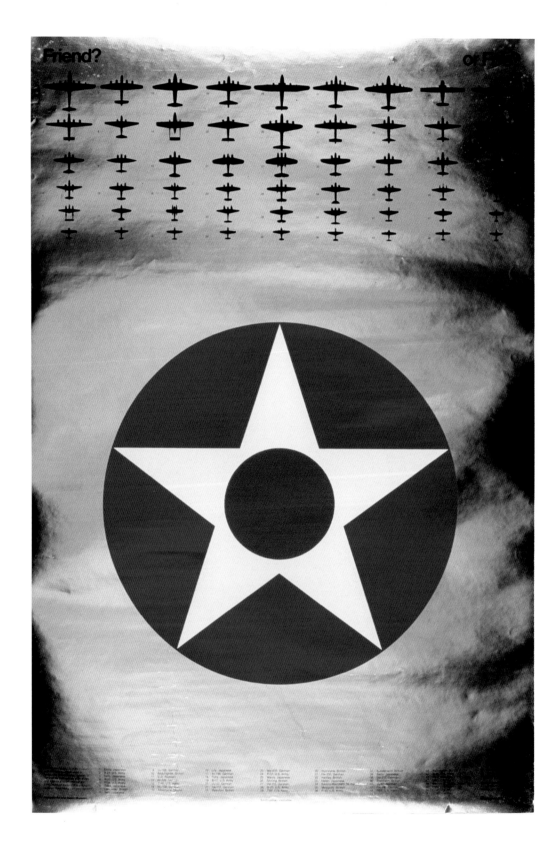

Friend? or F...

394

Extension of the Piccadilly Line to Heathrow Airport
now under construction

No. 0702
Miho Inc. (Tomoko Miho,
b. 1931, and James N.
Miho, b.1933)
Friend? or Foe?, 1975
National Air and Space
Museum, Washington, D.C.

No. 0703
Tom Eckersley (1914-1997)
*Extension of the Piccadilly
Line to Heathrow Airport*,
1971
London Transport Executive

No. 0704
Bruno Monguzzi (b. 1941)
*Majakovskij, Mejerchold,
Stanislavskij* (exhibition
poster), 1975
Castello Sforzesco, Milan

No. 0705
Makoto Nakamura (b. 1926)
Shiseido Flash Eyes, 1973
Japan

No. 0712
Artist unknown
Slash & Cut, c. 1975
UK
78.5 x 53.5 cm

No. 0713
Herbert Leupin
(1916-1999)
SSB Super, 1978
Swiss Railways

No. 0714
Tejo Hollander (b. 1942)
Heineken, c. 1975
The Netherlands
118 x 83 cm

No. 0715
Edward David Byrd
(b. 1941)
Jesus Christ Superstar, 1971
UK
76 x 40.5 cm

399

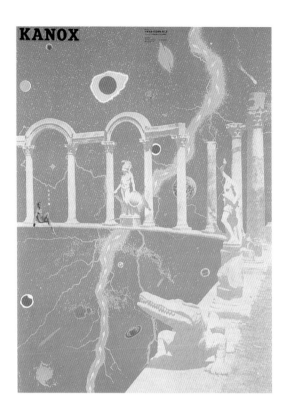

402

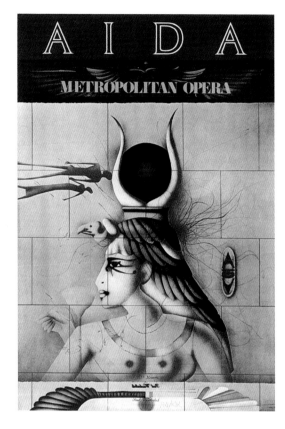

No. 0719

Tadanori Yokoo (b. 1936)
Kanox (media production
company), c. 1979
Japan
105.5 x 73 cm

No. 0720

Claude Kuhn-Klein
(b. 1948)
Artenschutz (poster for
World Wildlife Fund), 1985
Albin Uldry, Bern
70 x 100 cm

No. 0721

Paul Wunderlich (b. 1927)
Aïda, 1978
USA
91.5 x 61 cm

No. 0722

Ernst Volland (b. 1946)
Deutschland: Wir Kommen
(Germany: we're coming)
c. 1975
Wohlthatse Buchhandlung,
Berlin
88 x 62 cm

DEUTSCHLAND WIR KOMMEN

403

404

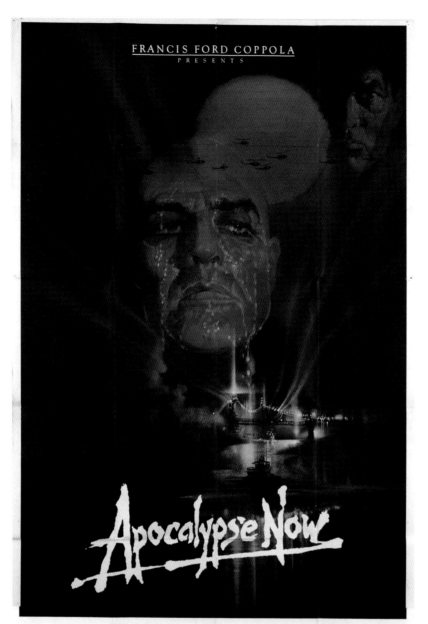

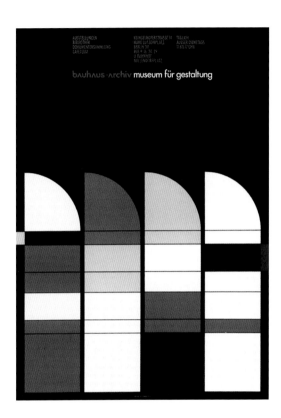

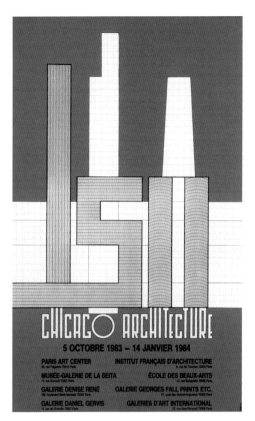

No. 0723
Bob Peak (1927-1992)
Apocalypse Now (movie
poster), 1979
USA
104 x 195 cm

No. 0724
Ott + Stein (Nicolaus Ott,
b. 1947, and Bernard Stein,
b. 1949)
Bauhaus-archiv, c. 1980
Berlin
59.5 x 84 cm

No. 0725
Tomislav
150: Chicago Architecture
(exhibition poster), 1983
France
49 x 81 cm

No. 0726
Steff Geissbühler (b. 1942)
Aiga/New York, 1987
USA
61 x 91.5 cm

406

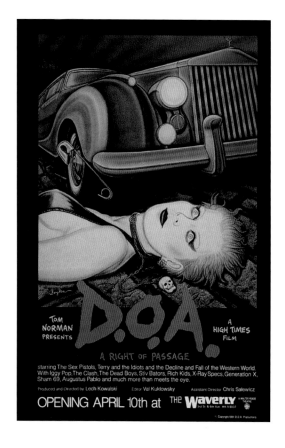

No. 0727
Soyka
D.O.A. (movie poster), 1981
USA
88.5 x 59 cm

No. 0728
Artist unknown
Brezhnev, 1981
USSR
67 x 49 cm

No. 0729
Saul Steinberg (1914-1999)
The New Yorker, 1976
The New Yorker Magazine,
Inc., New York
106.5 x 74 cm

407

408

No. 0730

Opland (Rob Wout)
(1928-2001)
Ga stemmen (Go vote . . .
against nuclear weapons in
Europe), 1981
The Netherlands
61 x 43 cm

No. 0731

Bernard Villemot
(1911-1989)
Bally, 1982
AK, Paris
119 x 83 cm

No. 0732

Jan Mlodozeniec
(1929-2000)
Fredro (theater poster),
1978
Poland

410

411

No. 0733
Volker Pfüller (b. 1939)
Dantons Tod (theater
poster), 1981
Deutsches Theater, Berlin

No. 0734
Volker Pfüller (b. 1939)
Der entfeffette Wotan
(theater poster), 1980
Deutsches Theater, Berlin
84 x 59 cm

No. 0735
Volker Pfüller (b. 1939)
Baal (theater poster), 1982
Deutsche Staatsoper, Berlin

412

413

No. 0736
Niklaus Troxler (b. 1947)
McCoy Tyner Sextet, 1980
Switzerland

No. 0737
Wim Crouwel (b. 1928)
The New Architecture
(exhibition poster), 1982
Architectural Institute,
Amsterdam

No. 0738
Alex Steinweiss (b. 1917)
Sarasota Jazz Festival, 1984
USA

414

No. 0739
Wild Plakken
Pasgeboren kunst (Newborn art, rude and demanding, not only speaks but screams: poster for a cultural center), 1984
Amsterdam
100 x 70 cm

No. 0740
Milton Glaser (b. 1929)
San Diego Jazz Festival, 1984
USA
61 x 91.5 cm

No. 0741
Heinz Edelmann (b. 1934)
Theater der Welt (poster for a theater festival), 1981
Cologne

No. 0742
Shigeo Fukuda (b. 1932)
Look 1 (exhibition poster), 1984
Japan

LOOK 1（万国旗のモナリザ・世界からの微笑） 1984

418

No. 0746
John Massey (b. 1931)
Connections (poster for the
Simpson Paper Company),
1985
USA

No. 0747
Artist unknown
Andy Warhol Marilyn 1967,
1989
Nouvelles Images Andy
Warhol Collection, France
70 x 85 cm

No. 0748
Heinz Edelmann (b. 1934)
Poster for *Cabaret*, 1986
Düsseldorfer
Schauspielhaus, Düsseldorf

No. 0749
Henryk Tomaszewski
(1914-2005)
Teresa Pagowska
(exhibition poster), 1988
Poland

teresa
Pągowska

Wystawa
Malarstwa

Galeria
Sztuki BWA
Gdańsk
Długa 67/68

Październik
1986

419

第一回国民文化祭 グランドフィナーレ

ありがとう・日本のこころ

閉会式
第一部 大学生合唱サークルとダークダックスとの競演
第二部 ハイブリッドコンサート
林英哲、鼓童相互の援助出演を得てジョイント演奏
昭和六十一年十一月二十九日土 午後二時開演
会場 国立劇場大劇場 東京都千代田区隼町四―一
主催 文化庁・東京都 入場無料

420

No. 0750
Ikko Tanaka (1930-2002)
Poster for the National
Cultural Festival, 1986
Japan

A GLOBAL EXCHANGE OF IDEAS

During the last two decades of the twentieth century, the advance of computer technology radically affected the course of graphic design. A multifaceted and pluralistic society of cultural diversity generated a global exchange of ideas combined with national visions. Countries where designers developed unique national approaches to design include the United Kingdom, Japan, and the Netherlands.

After World War II, British graphic designers assimilated both the rigidity of the International Style and the graphic expressionism of the New York School, while at the same time forging their own direction. Although Western graphic design influences, particularly the legacy of Constructivism, were clearly evident in Japanese poster design after 1945, designers in Japan managed to preserve their own traditions. Yusaku Kamekura was a leading figure in Japanese graphic design following the war. In his posters for the 1964 Tokyo Olympics he employed the design principles of Constructivism and the International Style, while drawing upon the poetic impulse of Japanese art. Western influences are also evident in the posters of Tadanori Yokoo, but instead of the structural approach of the International Style, Yokoo used mass media, pop art, and comic-book techniques as sources. The discarding of all tradition in his unconstrained posters has served to make him a cult figure in Japanese poster design. Late twentieth-century designers and studios in the Netherlands, such as Anthon Beeke, Studio Dumbar, Hard Werken, and Wild Plakken, rejected traditional values and sought highly personal graphic design solutions.

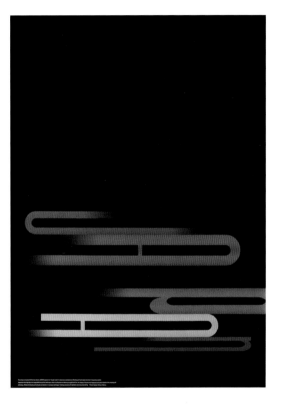

421

No. 0751
Minoru Niijima (b. 1948)
Japan (exhibition poster), 1988
Japan

422

No. 0752

Kazumasa Nagai (b. 1929)
Japan, 1987
Japan

No. 0753

Tapani Aartomaa (b. 1934)
Neljäs Vempula (exhibition
poster), 1988
Poster Museum, Lahti,
Finland

No. 0754

Werner Jeker (b. 1944)
Le Corbusier (exhibition
poster), 1987
Switzerland

No. 0755

Werner Jeker (b. 1944)
Man Ray (exhibition
poster), 1988
Switzerland

426

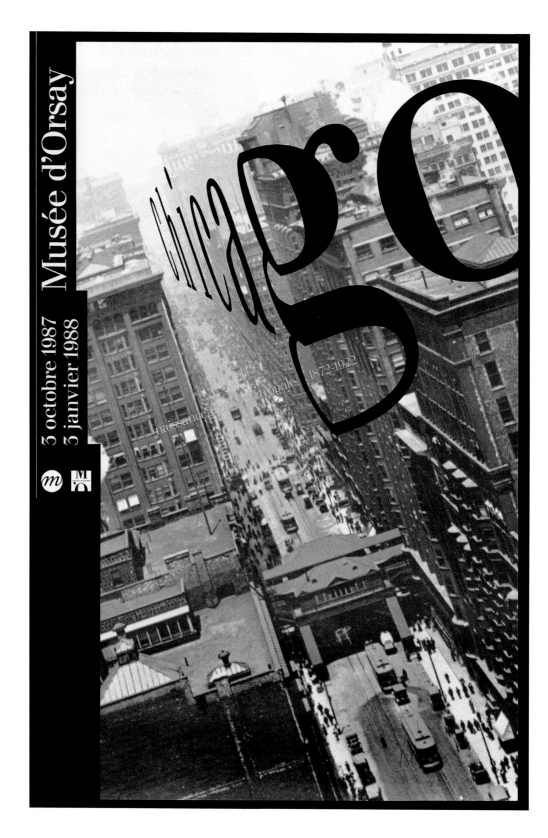

Musée d'Orsay

3 octobre 1987
3 janvier 1988

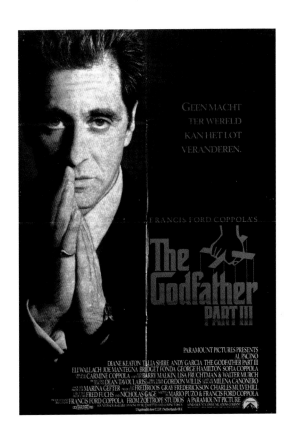

No. 0762
Philippe Apeloig (b. 1962)
Chicago (exhibition poster),
1987
Musée d'Orsay, Paris

No. 0763
Dawn Patrol
The Godfather, Part III
(movie poster), 1990
USA
70 x 102 cm

No. 0764
Fernando Medina
(b. 1945)
NEOCON 22, 1990
USA

No. 0765
Ben Faydherbe (b. 1958)
Film and Architecture (film
festival poster), 1987
The Netherlands

No. 0766

René Put and Irma Boom
(b. 1960)
Holland Festival, 1990
The Netherlands

No. 0767

Ralph Schraivogel (b. 1960)
Henry van de Velde
(exhibition poster), 1993
Museum für Gestaltung,
Zürich

No. 0768

Hard Werken (Willem Kars
and Gerard Hadders)
*19th Film Festival
Rotterdam*, 1990
The Netherlands
118 x 84 cm

No. 0769

Minoru Niijima (b. 1948)
*Emerging Japanese
Architects of the 1990s*
(exhibition poster),
c. 1990-91
USA

Emerging Japanese Architects of the 1990s

Featuring works by: Kunihi Say Takeyama / AMORPHE, Norihiko Dan, Hiroyuki Wakabayashi, WORKSHOP Hisashi Hara, Atsushi Kitagawara. Curated by Jackie Kestenbaum.
14 September–3 November 1990. Miriam and Ira D. Wallach Art Gallery, Department of Art History and Archaeology, Schermerhorn Hall 8th floor. Columbia University in the City of New York, New York, New York, 10027. Tel 212 854–7288. Hours: Wednesday–Saturday 1–5 p.m.
15 April–20 June 1991. Canadian Centre for Architecture, 1920 rue Baile, Montréal, Québec, Canada H3H 2S6. Tel 514 939–7020.
This exhibition has been made possible through the generous support of: The Japan Foundation, GRAHAM FOUNDATION, Yamada Shomei Lighting Co., Ltd., PLUS Corporation, and Asahi Glass Co., Ltd.
This exhibition is supported by the Consulate General of Japan at New York, and the Embassy of Canada in Japan. Coordinated by Ikuo Ogitsu. Assisted by Akiko Ogawa.
Special thanks to FUJISANKEI COMMUNICATIONS INTERNATIONAL, INC.

429

430

KAZUMASA NAGAI EXHIBITION
MAY15—JUNE3, 1991 DESIGN GALLERY, MATSUYA GINZA

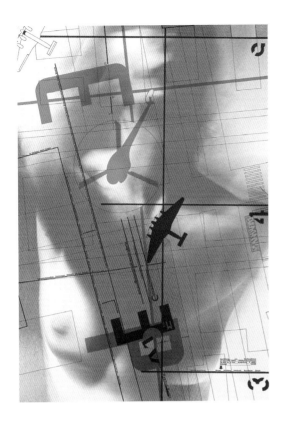

No. 0770
Kazumasa Nagai (b. 1929)
Kazumasa Nagai
(exhibition poster), 1991
Japan

No. 0771
Cyan (Detlef Fiedler,
b. 1955, Daniela Haufe,
b. 1966, et al.)
Magmec Berlin (exhibition
poster), 1992
Bauhaus Dessau, Germany

No. 0772
Cyan (Detlef Fiedler,
b. 1955, Daniela Haufe,
b. 1966, et al.)
Bauhaus Dessau (exhibition
poster), 1993
Bauhaus Dessau, Germany

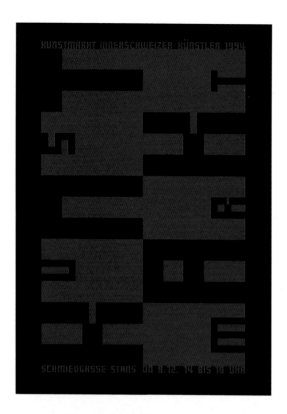

432

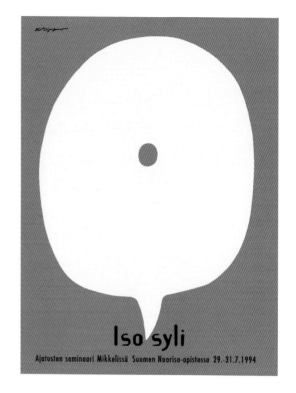

No. 0773
Melchior Imboden (b. 1956)
Kunstmarkt (poster for an
art fair), 1994
Switzerland

No. 0774
Tomi Ungerer (b. 1931)
*Montreux XXVII–Jazz
Festival*, 1993
Albin Uldry, Bern
70 x 100 cm

No. 0775
Kari Piippo (b. 1945)
Iso Syli (poster for a
seminar), 1994
Finland
70 x 100 cm

No. 0776
Lex Reitsma (b. 1958)
Wozzeck (opera poster),
1994
The Netherlands

De NEDER
LANDSE
OPERA
Het MUZIEKTHEATER
AMSTERDAM

WOZZECK

ALBAN BERG

27
30
4
6
9
13
15
18
21
24

PLAATSBESPREKEN 020 - 6 255 455
JAN FEBR 1994 20.00 UUR MATINEE 13.30 UUR

433

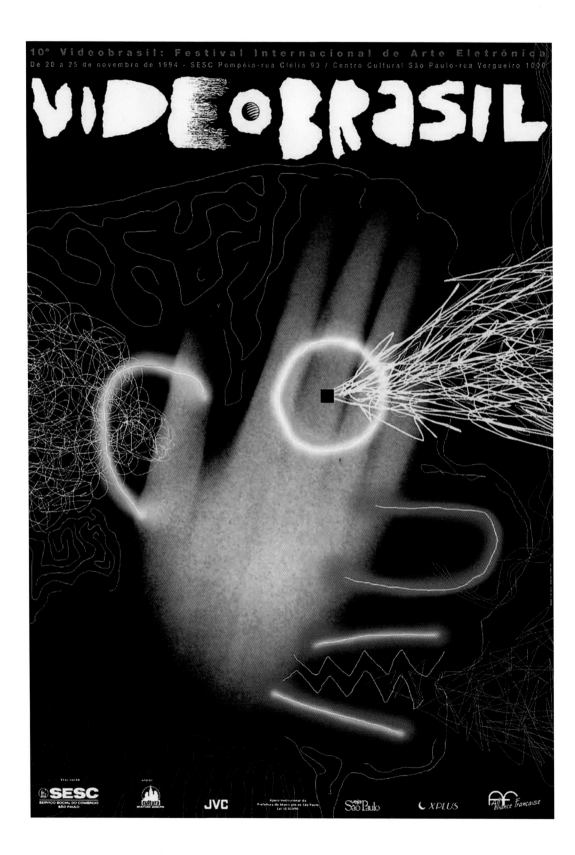

434

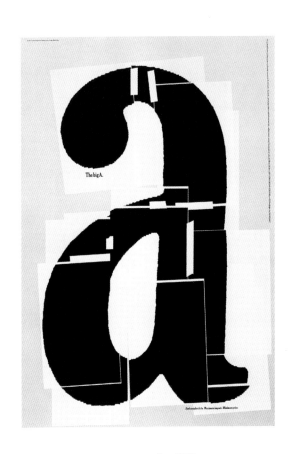

435

No. 0777

Kiko Farkas
Videobrasil, 1994
Brazil

No. 0778

Paula Scher (b. 1948)
The Big A (poster for a
printing company), 1991
USA

No. 0779

Tapani Aartomaa
(1934–2009)
Rzeszów (exhibition
poster), 1995
Poland

No. 0780

Koichi Sato (b. 1944)
Plakate aus Japan
(exhibition poster), 1993
Albin Uldry, Bern
90 x 128 cm

436

No. 0781
Paula Scher (b. 1948)
Simpatico (theater poster),
1994
USA

No. 0782
Frieder Grindler (b. 1941)
Othello (theater poster),
1994
Germany

No. 0783
Georges Calame
(1930-1999)
Tagliabue (poster for a
furniture store), 1994
Switzerland

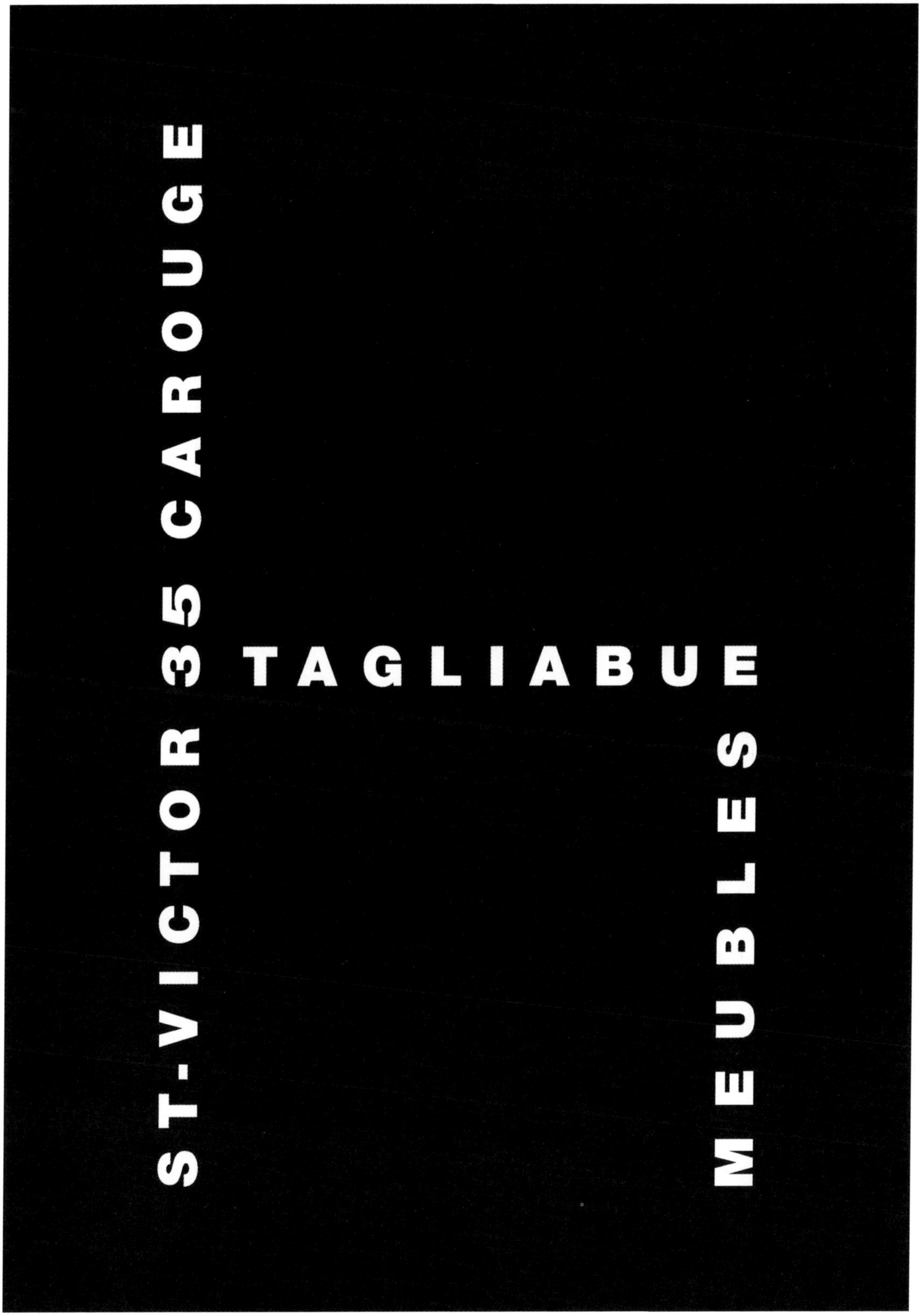

ST-VICTOR 35 CAROUGE

TAGLIABUE

MEUBLES

14.1. -
10.4.'94

made in
Holland

Design
aus den
Nieder-
landen

Museum für Angewandte Kunst Köln
An der Rechtschule, 50667 Köln
Dienstags bis Freitags 10-16 Uhr
Samstags und Sonntags 11-16 Uhr

438

Stadt Köln

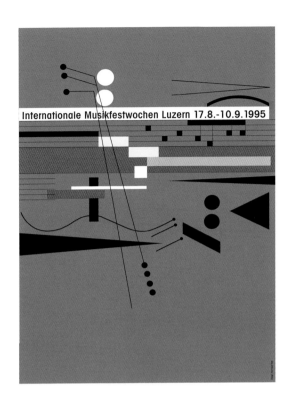

439

No. 0784
Loek Kemming (b. 1951)
Made in Holland (exhibition
poster), 1994
Germany

No. 0785
Rosmarie Tissi (b. 1937)
*Internationale
Musikfestwochen Lucerne*,
1995
Switzerland

No. 0786
Paula Scher (b. 1948)
*The Public Theater 95-96
Season*, 1995
USA

440

No. 0787
Keizo Matsui (b. 1946)
Women of the Century
(exhibition poster), 1994
Japan
73 x 103 cm

No. 0788
Peter Scholl
Compagnie Nomades (ballet
poster), c. 1995
Switzerland
90.5 x 128 cm

No. 0789
Robert & Durrer
Bill (poster for a Max Bill
exhibition), 1998
Switzerland
90 x 128 cm

No. 0790
Anthon Beeke (b. 1940)
Once Upon a Time
(exhibition poster), 1991
Switzerland
83 x 118 cm

No. 0791
Uwe Loesch (b. 1943)
Hommage aan Antwerpen,
1993
Belgium
84 x 119 cm

442

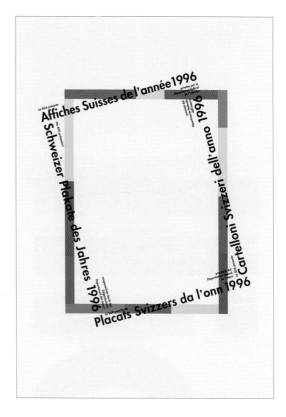

No. 0792
Alexander Gelman (b. 1967)
Biblios (poster for poetry
readings), 1995
USA

No. 0793
Rosmarie Tissi (b. 1937)
Affiches Suisses de l'année
(exhibition poster), 1996
Switzerland

No. 0794
Dimitris Arvanitis (b. 1948)
Radio Moscow (movie
poster), 1995
Greece

Radio MOSCOW ★

A FILM BY NICHOLAS TRIANDAFYLLIDIS

Music by
Blaine L. Reinenger

Production
Greek Film Centre
ASTRA [vision & sound]

ANT 1 TV
Nico Vergelis

1 4* 7 10 13 16 20 23 27 30
juni 95 17.30 / *13.30 uur
Die Meistersinger von Nürnberg
Richard Wagner
produktie in het kader van het Holland Festival
De Nederlandse Opera
Het MUZIEKTHEATER
AMSTERDAM

444

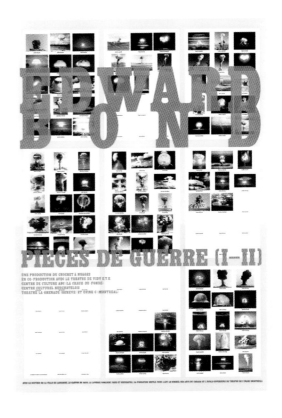

No. 0795
Lex Reitsma (b. 1958)
Die Meistersinger von Nürnberg (opera poster), 1995
The Netherlands

No. 0796
André Baldinger (b. 1963)
ANCT: Atelier National de Création Typographique, 1993
France

No. 0797
André Baldinger (b. 1963)
Edward Bond: Pièces de Guerre (theater poster), 2003
Switzerland

No. 0798
Domenic K. Geissbühler (b. 1932)
Zürcher Ballett, 1995
Switzerland
90 x 128 cm

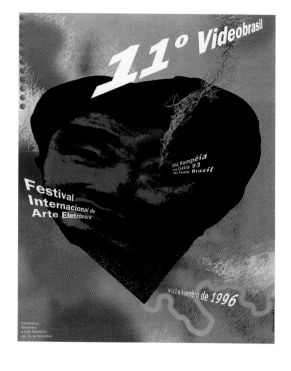

No. 0803
Alexander Gelman (b. 1967)
Poster of the Side watch
from Swatch, 1996
USA

No. 0804
Chen Shaohua (b. 1954)
"Communication"
(exhibition poster), 1996
China

No. 0805
Kiko Farkas
11th Videobrasil, 1996
Brazil

No. 0806
Jennifer Morla (b. 1955)
El Museo Mexicano, 1995
USA

EL MUSEO
MEXICANO

celebrating twenty years of art and culture

flux:

the edinburgh new music festival

1st week

jaffa cake 8/97

tue/wed the divine comedy
12/13 with michael nyman
thurs 14 the wannadies
fri 15 andy sheppard/jazz jamaica
sat 16 babybird
sun 17 strike out 4 (at 13.00)
doors 20.00
tickets fringe 0131 226 5138
inside tickets 0131 477 8222
a usp arts presentation

No. 0807

Hamish Muir
*Flux: The Edinburgh New
Music Festival*, 1997
UK

No. 0808

Cyan (Detlef Fiedler,
b. 1955, Daniela Haufe,
b. 1966, et al.)
Singuhr-hoergalerie (audio-
visual exhibition space),
1997
Berlin

No. 0809

Cyan (Detlef Fiedler,
b. 1955, Daniela Haufe,
b. 1966, et al.)
Cie. Toula Limnaios (poster
for dance company), 1998
Germany

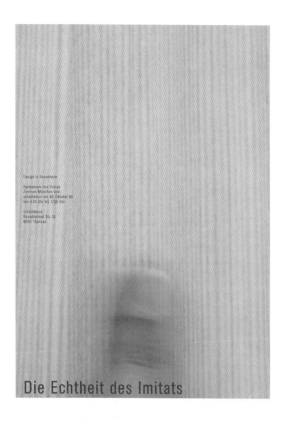

Die Echtheit des Imitats

452

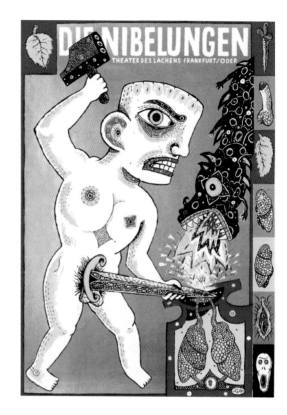

No. 0810
Gerwin Schmidt (b. 1966)
Die Echtheit des Imitats
(poster for a design
symposium), 1998
Germany

No. 0811
Celestino Piatti (b. 1922)
*100 Jahre Basler Tier
Schutz Verein*, 1997
Switzerland

No. 0812
Georg Barber (b. 1967)
Die Nibelungen (theater
poster), 1997
Germany

No. 0813
Helmut Brade (b. 1937)
*Leben und Tod König
Richard des Dritten* (theater
poster), 1997
Germany

LEBEN UND TOD
KÖNIG RICHARD
DES DRITTEN
VON WILLIAM SHAKESPEARE
Musik: GÜNTHER FISCHER
Regie: MANFRED WEKWERTH
Bühnenbild: MANFRED GRUND
Kostüme: URSULA WOLF

nt
neues theater halle

453

Edinburgh Fringe, Aug 98

Flux

@Queen's Hall Clerk Street
Fri 14/Sat 15 Spiritualized &
Steve Martland. Sun 16 Ken
Kesey & Ken Babbs, Fri 21/
Sat 22 Nick Cave. Fri 28 John
Zorn. Sat 29 The Creatures.
@Jaffa Cake Grassmarket
Sun 16/Mon 17 The Jesus
& Mary Chain, Tue 18 Je t'aime
Gainsbourg, Thu 20 Roddy
Frame. Fri 21 The Bathers, Pearl
Fishers. The Swiss Family
Orbison. Sat 22 Arab Strap &
The Nectarine No 9. Sun 23
David Thomas & Yo La Tengo.
Tue 25 P J Harvey, Thu 27 Asian
Dub Foundation.
All doors 8pm
Tickets from £8
Box Office 0131 667 7776
A USP Arts Presentation

454

No. 0814
Hamish Muir
Flux, 1998
UK

No. 0815
Jennifer Morla (b. 1955)
Levi's, 1998
USA

No. 0816
Jacques Koeweiden
*Andre Agassi: Have Mercy.
Kill Quickly* (Nike ad
campaign), 1998

456

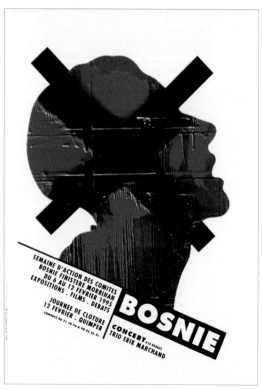

No. 0817
Tadanori Yokoo (b. 1936)
Tadanori Yokoo Exhibition,
1998
Japan
72 x 103 cm

No. 0818
Alain Le Quernec (b. 1944)
Bosnie, c. 1998
France

No. 0819
Domenic K. Geissbühler
(b. 1932)
*Balanchine Kylian Spoerli
Manen* (ballet poster), 1997
Switzerland
90 x 128 cm

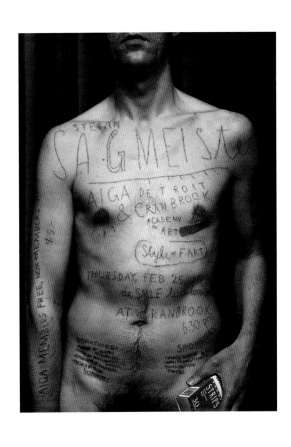

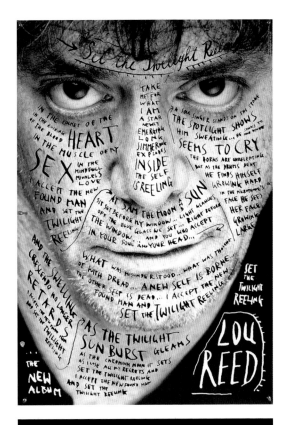

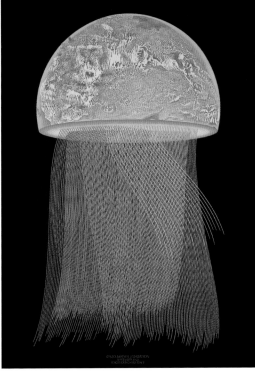

No. 0820

Stefan Sagmeister (b. 1962)
Stefan Sagmeister (AIGA
lecture poster), 1999
USA

No. 0821

Stefan Sagmeister (b. 1962)
Set the Twilight Reeling,
Lou Reed (poster for CD),
1996
USA

No. 0822

Keizo Matsui (b. 1946)
Keizo Matsui Exhibition,
1995
Japan

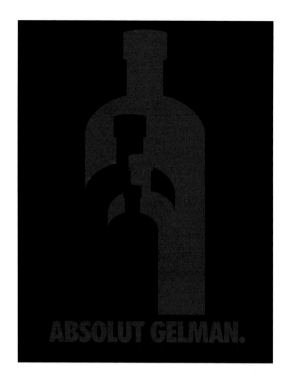

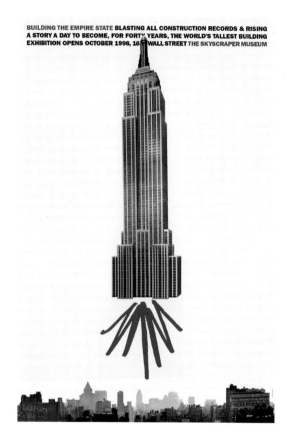

458

No. 0823
Alexander Gelman (b. 1967)
Absolut Gelman, 1998
USA

No. 0824
Bingnan Yu (b. 1933)
Family, c. 1998
China

No. 0825
Michael Gericke
Building the Empire State
(exhibition poster), 1998
USA

No. 0826
Georg Barber (b. 1967)
White Trash Carnival, 1998
Germany

459

LE CHAPEAU MELON

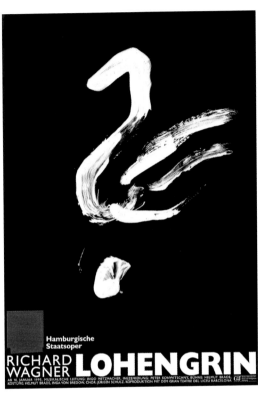

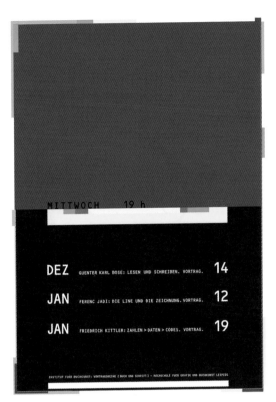

No. 0827
Santiago Pol (b. 1946)
Marcel Marceau: Le Chapeau Melon, 1999
Venezuela

No. 0828
Helmut Brade (b. 1937)
Lohengrin (opera poster), 1998
Germany

No. 0829
Günter Karl Bose (b. 1951)
Poster for lecture series, 1998
Germany

No. 0830
Kaoru Kasai (b. 1949)
The 4th Tokyo TDC Exhibition, 1992
Japan

Water
for
human
kind.

464

2000 Suric Design   Print: Lacalunitol   ●   Association pour une banque d'images   l'eau pour l'humanité

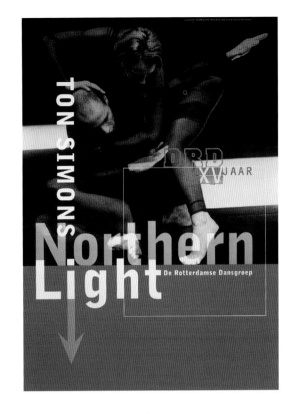

No. 0835
Yuri Surkov
Water for Human Kind,
2000
Russia

No. 0836
Lex Reitsma (b. 1958)
Capriccio (opera poster),
2000
The Netherlands

No. 0837
Wout de Vringer (b. 1959)
Northern Light (poster for a
dance group), 2000
The Netherlands

No. 0838
Paul Sahre
*Paul Sayer, Exercises in
Futility* (lecture poster),
2000
USA

ISSEY MIYAKE

No. 0839
Michael Mabry
AIGA, 2000
USA

No. 0840
Melchior Imboden (b. 1956)
Kunstmarkt Innerschweizer Künstler (poster for an art fair), 2000
Switzerland

No. 0841
Hideki Nakajima
Photo: Chikashi Suzuki
Issey Miyake, 2000
Japan

No. 0842
Giorgio Pesce
Les Urbaines (poster for an arts festival for young people), 2000
Switzerland

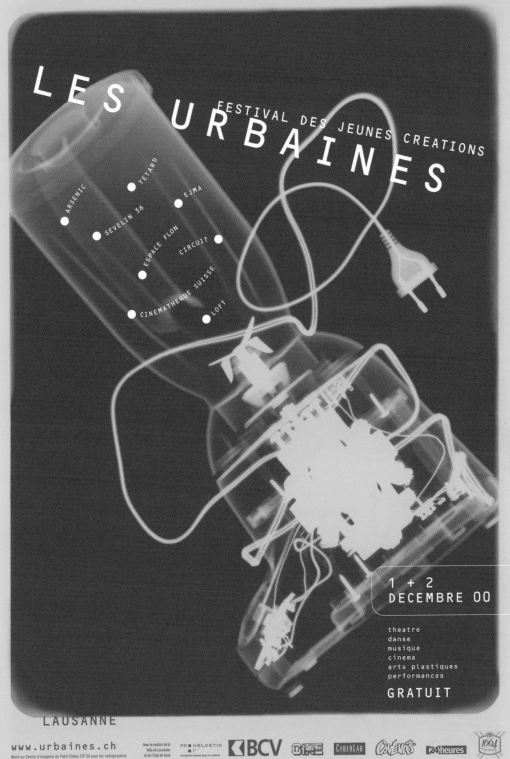

467

468

Crafts Council Gallery
44a Pentonville Road
Islington, London N1 9BY
Tel 020 7278 7700
5 minutes from Angel tube

Free entry
Tues to Sat 11-6
Sunday 2-6
Closed Monday
Disabled Access

Closed from 6.00
Saturday 23 December
Re-opens Tuesday
2 January 2001

FABRIC OF FASHION

CRAFTS COUNCIL GALLERY
9 NOVEMBER 2000 – 14 JANUARY 2001

A BRITISH COUNCIL EXHIBITION INCLUDING HUSSEIN CHALAYAN, CAROL FRASER,
ELEY KISHIMOTO, JESSICA OGDEN, UNIFORM, VEXED GENERATION

The British Council

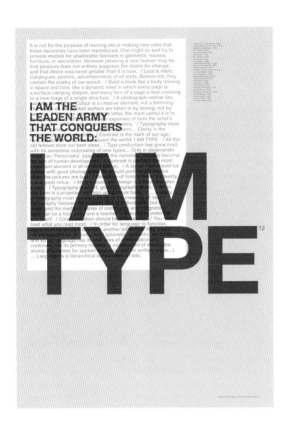

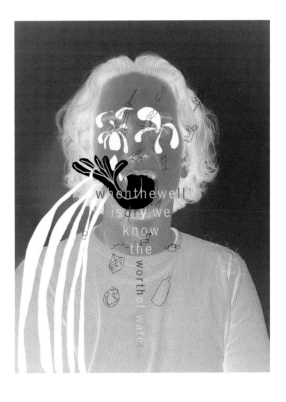

No. 0843
Angus Hyland
Fabric of Fashion
(exhibition poster), 2000
UK

No. 0844
Angus Hyland
*I Am the Leaden Army that
Conquers the World: I Am
Type*, c. 2000
UK

No. 0845
Bob van Dijk (b. 1967) and
Studio Dumbar
1:4, 2000
The Netherlands

No. 0846
Bob van Dijk (b. 1967) and
Studio Dumbar
*When the well is dry, we
know the worth of water*,
2000
The Netherlands

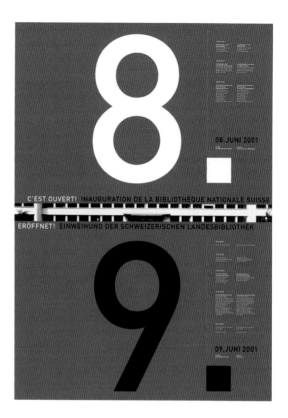

470

No. 0847
Stanley Wong (b. 1960)
Red Blue White (Rebuild
HK campaign), 2001
Hong Kong

No. 0848
Mihaly Varga
C'est ouvert! (poster for the
Swiss National Library),
2001
Switzerland

No. 0849
Fang Cao
Print-Seal (poster for an
exhibition of Chinese
character design), 1997
Nanking, China

471

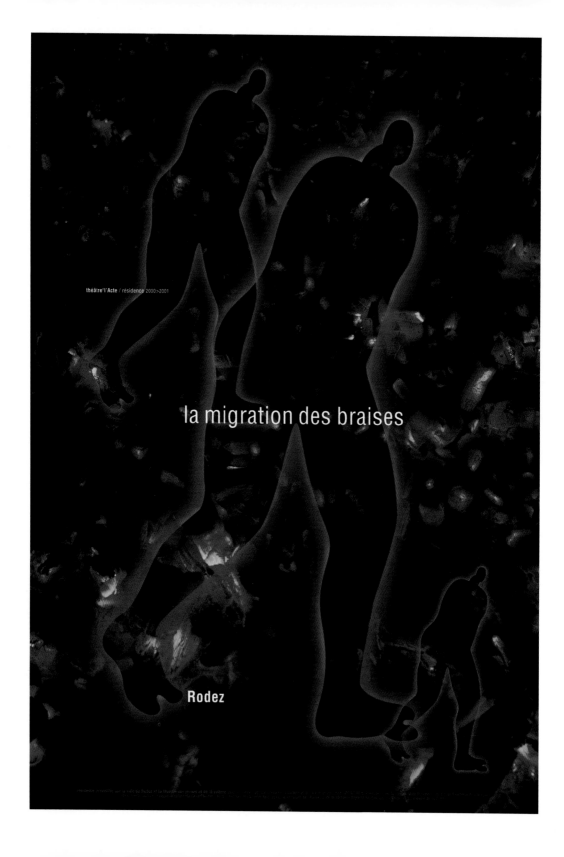

théâtre²l'Acte / résidence 2000>2001

la migration des braises

Rodez

No. 0850
Ronald Curchod (b. 1954)
La migration des braises
(theater poster), 2000
France

No. 0851
Tatsuo Ebina
TBS (Tokyo Broadcasting
System), 2000
Japan

No. 0852
Ralph Schraivogel (b. 1960)
Paul Newman, 2001
Zürich

No. 0853
Yasuhiro Sawada (b. 1961)
d. (exhibition poster: "The
Design Spirit of Japan"),
2001
Japan

474

No. 0854
Jacques Koeweiden
Winter de hortus, 2001
The Netherlands

No. 0855
Alejandro Magallanes
(b. 1971)
La Primera Vez (poster for
a film festival), 2001
Mexico

No. 0856
Catherine Zask (b. 1961)
Macbeth (theater poster),
2001
France

MACBETH

SHAKESPEARE

L'Hippodrome, scène nationale de Douai, est subventionné par le ministère de la Culture et de la Communication, la ville de Douai, la région Nord-Pas-de-Calais et le département du Nord · conception graphique Emmanuel Jaco · réalisation AMV · octobre 2001

475

L'HIPPODROME MERCREDI 7 NOVEMBRE 2001 À 20H30
JEUDI 8 NOVEMBRE À 19H
MISE EN SCÈNE **SYLVAIN MAURICE**
CRÉATION AVIGNON 2001
TÉL. 03 27 99 66 66

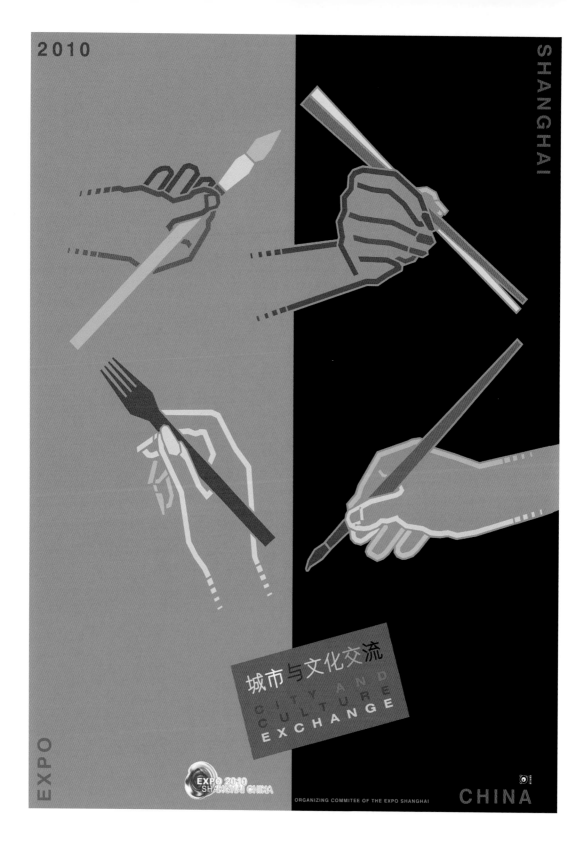

476

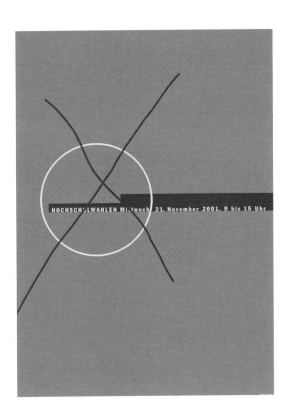

No. 0857
Santiago Pol (b. 1946)
Expo 2010 Shanghai, 2001
China

No. 0858
Helfried Hagenberg
Hochschulwahlen (poster
for a student election),
2001
Germany

No. 0859
Russell Warren-Fisher
Poster for *Printed Matter
No. 1*, 2002

478

No. 0860
Michel Lepetitdidier
(b. 1962)
Poster for the Théâtre de
la Manufacture, Nancy, c.
c. 2001
France

No. 0861
Makoto Nakamura (b. 1926)
Japan, 2001
Japan

No. 0862
K. Domenic Geissbühler
(b. 1932)
Maria Stuarda (theater
poster), 2002
Switzerland

MARIA

OPERNHAUS ZÜRICH

DONIZETTI

VIOTTI

ASAGAROFF/DEL MONACO

VÄISÄNEN

WALEK

KUNZ

HÄMMERLI

CHOR und ORCHESTER
der OPER ZÜRICH

UNTERSTÜTZT VON
DER CONFISERIE TEUSCHER

AB 7. DEZEMBER 2002

STUARDA

479

480

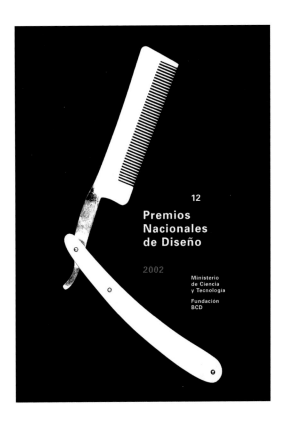

No. 0863

Cyan (Detlef Fiedler,
b. 1955, Daniela Haufe,
b. 1966, et al.)
Singuhr-hoergalerie (audio-
visual exhibition space),
2004
Berlin

No. 0864

Stephen Doyle (b. 1956)
Fresh Dialogue (poster for
an AIGA event), 2006
USA

No. 0865

Isidro Ferrer Soria
(b. 1963)
*Premios Nacionales de
Diseño*, 2002
Spain

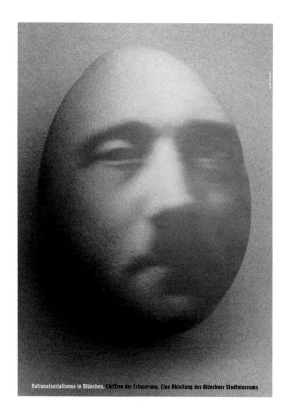

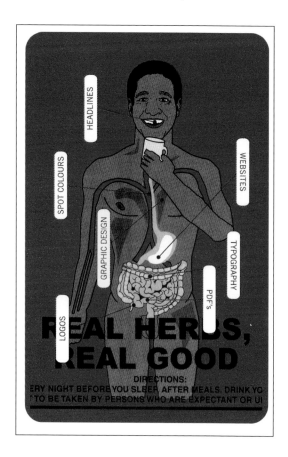

No. 0866
Gerwin Schmidt (b. 1966)
Nationalsozialismus in München (exhibition poster), 2002
Germany

No. 0867
Jacques Koeweiden
Masterclass, 2002
The Netherlands

No. 0868
Garth Walker
Real Herbs, Real Good, 2002
South Africa

No. 0869
Alejandro Magallanes
(b. 1971)
Detrás de la Fantasía Americana (Behind the American dream), 2001
Mexico

486

運転手は、きみだ。

インターネットは、ぼくへだ。

www.dion.ne.jp

488

LE TRIPTYQUE DE TIBERIADE DE JOSE SARAMAGO

THEATRE PAR LE CROCHET A NUAGES

GRANGE DE DORIGNY DU 3 AU 15 DECEMBRE

LOCATION 021 318 71 71 OU 021 692 21 12

AVEC LE SOUTIEN DE LA VILLE DE LAUSANNE — LA FONDATION NESTLE POUR L'ART — LA LOTERIE ROMANDE

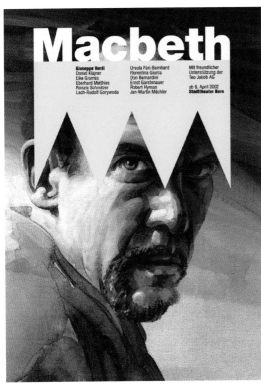

No. 0878

André Baldinger (b. 1963)
Le Triptyque de Tiberiade
(theater poster), 2002
Switzerland

No. 0879

Stephan Bundi (b. 1950)
Macbeth (opera poster),
2002
Switzerland

No. 0880

Günter Karl Bose (b. 1951)
Musica Viva (poster for a
concert series), 2002
Germany

No. 0881

Tapani Aartomaa
(1934-2009)
Doping (antidrugs poster),
2002
Finland

490

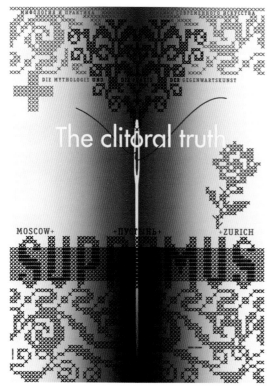

No. 0882
Henning Wagenbreth
(b. 1962)
Jazzfest Berlin, 2003
Germany

No. 0883
Yuri Surkov
Supremus (poster for an art project), 2003

No. 0884
Catherine Zask (b. 1961)
Blush (poster for a dance performance), 2003
France

No. 0885
Martin Woodtli (b. 1971)
VideoEx (exhibition poster), 2003
Switzerland

491

No. 0886
Paula Scher (b. 1948)
Fucking A (theater poster),
2003
USA

No. 0887
Stefan Sagmeister (b. 1962)
*Adobe Design Achievement
Awards*, 2003
USA

No. 0888
Minoru Niijima (b. 1948)
Musashino Art University,
2003
Japan

THE POSTER AS A PERSONAL ARTISTIC EXPRESSION

As we move forward into the twenty-first century, an age of constantly changing technology and instant gratification, the poster assumes new forms. The demise of the printed book was often envisaged as far back as the 1960s, yet in spite of the Kindle, and now the iPad, it continues to thrive. The same dire prediction has been made about the poster, but it too will prove resilient. As the Bulgarian born Luba Lukova aptly stated, "Posters bring a kind of humanness and emotion that screen based media can't provide."

The poster continues to flourish in many parts of the world as an important visual communication medium. Its basic form remains essentially the same as it was one hundred and fifty years ago. Although far more refined and faster, lithographic printing has changed very little since it was invented at the end of the eighteenth century. Yet new computer advances have become an integral part of the graphic-design process and have opened up endless new vistas for contemporary poster designers. However, the basic goal has not changed: A poster still presents a product, a viewpoint, or an event. In a period when we are saturated daily with a plethora of images, it is even more critical that a poster seize a viewer's attention.

Posters maintain the purest form of graphic communication, and designers such as Paula Scher, Ralph Schraivogel, and Stefan Sagmeister have provided new paradigms. We are now confronted with a wide range of styles, and there are no longer the obvious trends that were dominant for most of the twentieth century.

Today's digital technology allows for limited, short-run exclusive posters, which often showcase some of the most creative work being produced today. With this technology, poster designers have more room to experiment and take risks, providing a unique venue for the artist's personal artistic expression. And while the poster is still a printed piece, artists now have the tools of digital communication to share their art and collaborate with other artists throughout the world.

493

498

499

No. 0895
Rudi Meyer
De Berlioz à Broadway
(theater poster), 2003
France

No. 0896
Michel Bouvet, (b. 1955)
Photographie Arles, 2003
France

No. 0897
Bob van Dijk (b. 1967),
NLXL
Culture Night, 2003
The Netherlands

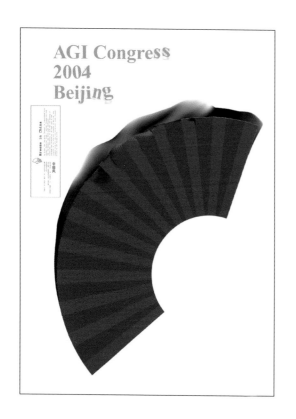

No. 0898
Jian Zhao
Breeze in China (poster
for graphic design
conference), 2004
Beijing

No. 0899
Günter Karl Bose (b. 1951)
Musica Viva 2003/2004
(poster for a concert
series), 2003
Germany

No. 0900
Peter Bilak (b. 1973)
Trnava Poster Triennial,
2003
Slovakia

OULIPO

→ OULIPO

EINE VERANSTALTUNG DES LITERATURHAUSES BERLIN → AM 20. MAI
OULIPOESIE → AM 21. MAI OULIPROSE → AM 22. MAI OULISTOIRE → MIT
MARCEL BÉNABOU → ANNE GARRÉTA → JACQUES JOUET → HERVÉ LE
TELLIER → IAN MONK → OSKAR PASTIOR → JACQUES ROUBAUD → OLIVIER
SALON → JÜRGEN RITTE [MODERA
TION] → GEFÖRDERT DURCH DIE
FRANZÖSISCHE BOTSCHAFT UND
DAS INSTITUT FRANÇAIS SOWIE
MIT FREUNDLICHER UNTERSTÜT
ZUNG VON BERLINER PILSNER →

l i .

o u l i . p o

Foto: Imm. Leipzig Berlin

502

Literaturhaus Berlin Fasanenstrasse 23 Berlin Charlottenburg

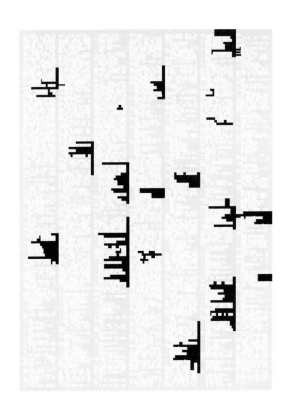

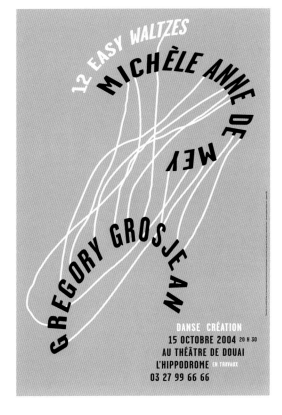

503

No. 0901
Günter Karl Bose (b. 1951)
Oulipo (poster for a literary
event), 2003
Germany

No. 0902
Catherine Zask (b. 1961)
Alcibiade au Téléphone,
2000
France

No. 0903
Catherine Zask (b. 1961)
12 Easy Waltzes (poster
for a dance performance),
2004
France

504

No. 0904
Martin Woodtli (b. 1971)
Lichtecht (exhibition
poster), 2004
Switzerland

No. 0905
Wout de Vringer (b. 1959)
Museon, 2004
The Netherlands

No. 0906
Leonardo Sonnoli
(b. 1962)
Lina Bo Bardi (exhibition
poster), 2004
Italy

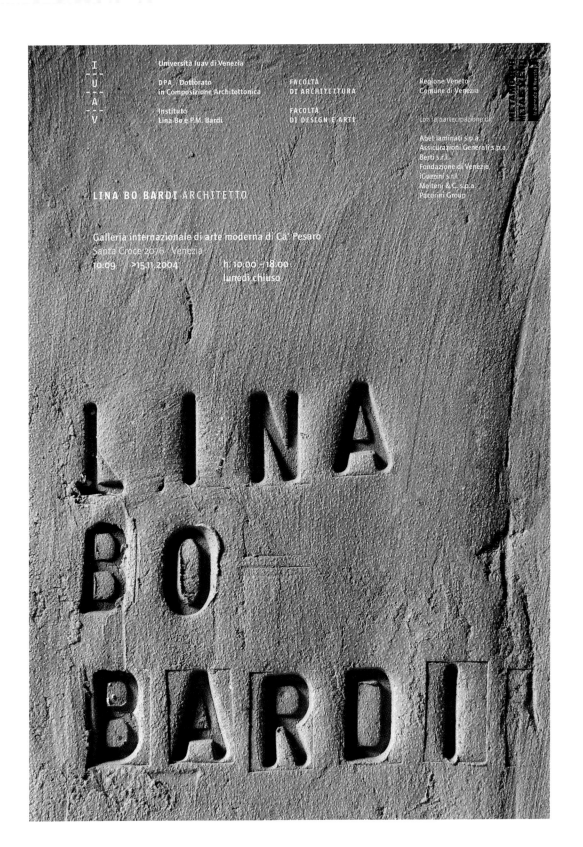

Università Iuav di Venezia

D.P.A. - Dottorato
in Composizione Architettonica

FACOLTÀ
DI ARCHITETTURA

Istituto
Lina Bo e P.M. Bardi

FACOLTÀ
DI DESIGN E ARTI

Regione Veneto
Comune di Venezia

Con la partecipazione di

Abet laminati s.p.a.
Assicurazioni Generali s.p.a.
Berti s.r.l.
Fondazione di Venezia
iGuzzini s.r.l.
Molteni & C. s.p.a.
Pacorini Group

LINA BO BARDI ARCHITETTO

Galleria internazionale di arte moderna di Ca' Pesaro
Santa Croce 2076 Venezia
10.09   >15.11.2004   h. 10.00 –18.00
                               lunedì chiuso

505

No. 0910
Sabina Oberholzer and
Renato Tagli
Omaggio a Joseph Beuys
(exhibition poster series),
2004
Switzerland

509

510

No. 0911

Rudi Meyer
Chatelet Saison 2004-2005
(theater poster), 2004
France

No. 0912

Peter Moser
*Du sollst den Namen des
Herrn* (opera poster: *Die
Nibelungen*), 2004
Germany

No. 0913

Shinnoske Sugisaki
(b. 1953)
Poster for the Mana Screen
silkscreen company, 2004
Japan

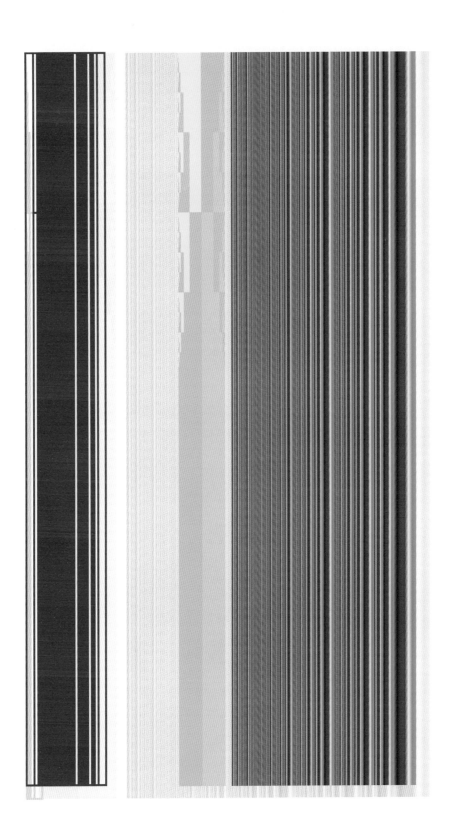

511

Seven Intellectuals
In Bamboo Forest
2003 Part 1

Director : Yang Fudong
Music: Jin Wang
Design: Jianping He

512

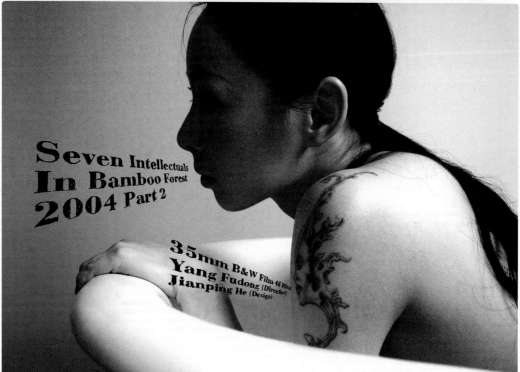

Seven Intellectuals
In Bamboo Forest
2004 Part 2

35mm B&W Film 46 Mins.
Yang Fudong (Director)
Jianping He (Design)

No. 0914 / No. 0915

Jianping He
*Seven Intellectuals in
Bamboo Forest* (movie
posters), 2003/2004

No. 0916

Michael Mabry
Stop the Arrogance, 2004
USA

No. 0917

Helfried Hagenberg
Bilder aus der Wirtschaft
(lecture poster), 2004
Germany

18 ...
septembre
17 octobre
04
mois du patrimoine écrit
curiosités et éphémères

516

No. 0921

Michel Lepetitdidier
(b. 1962)
Curiosités et Éphémères
(exhibition poster), 2004
France

No. 0922

Cyan (Detlef Fiedler
b. 1955, Daniela Haufe,
b. 1966, et al.)
*Urban+Aboriginal XVI. Alte
und neue Musik aus Korea*
(concert poster), 2004
Germany

No. 0923

Helmut Feliks Büttner
(b. 1940)
Willem Breuker Kollektief
(concert poster), 2004
The Netherlands

518

No. 0924
Stephan Bundi (b. 1950)
Boccaccio (opera poster),
2004
Switzerland

No. 0925
Ebrahim Haghighi (b. 1949)
Sadeq Hedayat 1903-1950
(tribute to an Iranian
writer), 2004
Iran

No. 0926
Anette Lenz and Vincent
Perrottet
La Tête dans les Nuages
(poster for a theater
festival), 2004
France

LA TÊTE DANS LES NUAGES

DU
28
MARS
AU
4 AVRIL
2004

FESTIVAL
DE
SPECTACLES
POUR
LES
ENFANTS
ET
LEURS
PARENTS

05
45
38
61
62

Theatre
SCENE NATIONALE
d'Angouleme

519

Christopher Marlowe

DOKTOR FAUSTUS

The Tragicall History of the horrible Life and Death of Doctor Faustus
in der Übersetzung und Bearbeitung von Manfred WEKWERTH

Regie: Manfred Wekwerth.   Bühnenbild und Kostüme: Rolf Klemm.   Musik: Syman

Im Dom zu Halle.

Only this,
Gentleman,
we muft perform!
The form of
Fauftus fortunes
good and bad.
To patient
we appeal
our priaud.

Christopher
Marlowe
1589

520

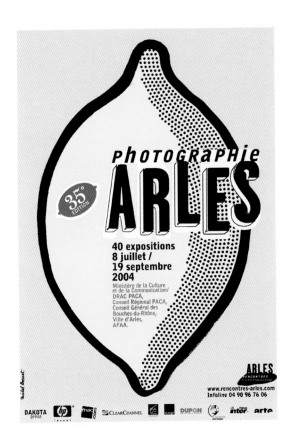

No. 0927
Helmut Brade (b. 1937)
Doktor Faustus (theater
poster), 2004
Germany

No. 0928
Michel Bouvet (b. 1955)
Photographie Arles, 2004
France

No. 0929
Anette Lenz and Vincent
Perrottet
La Tête dans les Nuages
(poster for a theater
festival), 2005
France

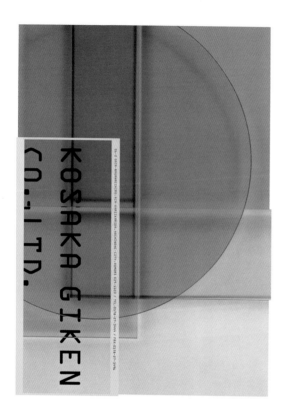

No. 0930

Yasuhiro Sawada (b. 1961)
Kosaka Giken (poster for
a construction company),
2004
Japan

No. 0931

Alejandro Magallanes
(b. 1971)
Muxe's (movie poster),
2005
Mexico

No. 0932

Reza Abedini (b. 1967)
*Iranian Culture Posters
Exhibition*, 2004
Iran

COLORS OF

SHENG

CRIMSON

♛ DON 6 EN VRIJ 7 OKT 05

CONCERTGEBOUWORKEST

DAVID ROBERTSON, DIRIGENT

TOMOKO MUKAIYAMA, PIANO COLIN CURRIE, SLAGWERK

WERKEN VAN STRAVINSKY, ANDRIESSEN,

SHENG EN HINDEMITH

ING Sara Lee D-E NUON PHILIPS

SPONSORS VAN HET KONINKLIJK CONCERTGEBOUWORKEST

TEL 020 671 83 45 » 0900 0191 » WWW.CONCERTGEBOUWORKEST.NL

524

No. 0933
René Knip (b. 1963)
Colors of Sheng Crimson
(concert poster), 2005
The Netherlands

No. 0934
René Knip (b. 1963)
Piano Concert Ullmann
(concert poster), 2005
The Netherlands

No. 0935
Jianping He (b. 1973)
Bilder-Schrift (exhibition
poster), 2005
Germany

No. 0936
Helmut Feliks Büttner
(b. 1940)
5. Jazz Band Ball, 2005
Germany

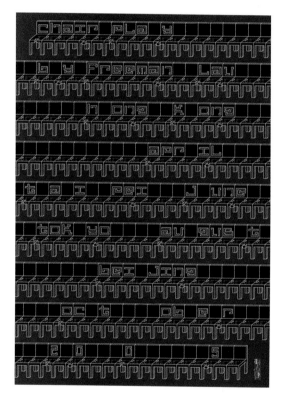

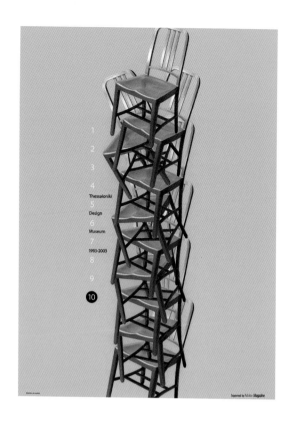

No. 0937
Freeman Lau (b. 1958)
Chairplay (exhibition
poster), 2005
Taipei

No. 0938
Dimitris Arvanitis (b. 1948)
10 (poster for the 10th
anniversary of the
Thessaloniki Design
Museum), 2004
Greece

No. 0939
David Pidgeon (b. 1972)
Anna Finlayson (exhibition
poster), 2004
Australia

527

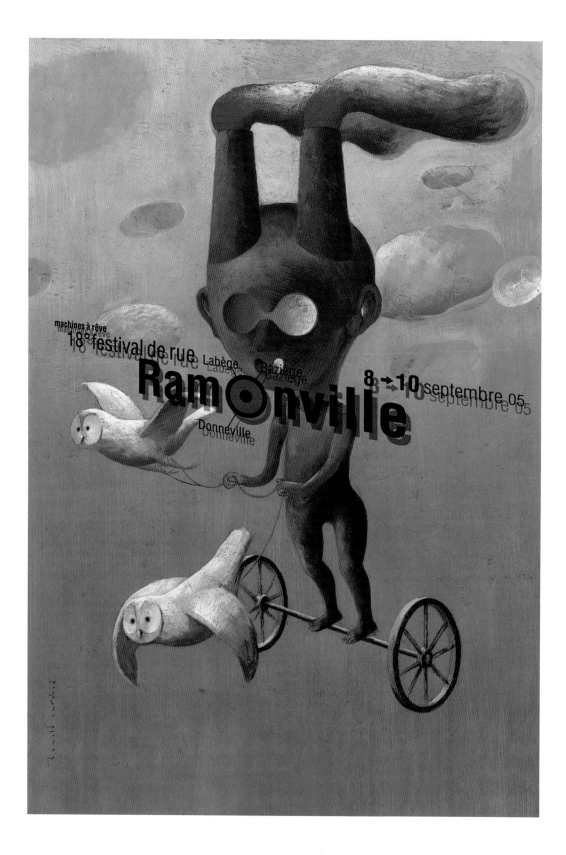

machines à rêve
18ᵉ festival de rue Labège Baziège
Ramonville 8 →10 septembre 05
Donneville

528

No. 0940

Ronald Curchod (b. 1954)
*18° festival de rue
Ramonville* (street-theater
festival), 2005
France

No. 0941

Walter Bohatsch
*Typographie – bauen mit
zeichen* (lecture poster),
2005
Austria

No. 0942

Walter Bohatsch
*Arnold Schönberg: Der
Maler* (exhibition poster),
2005
Austria

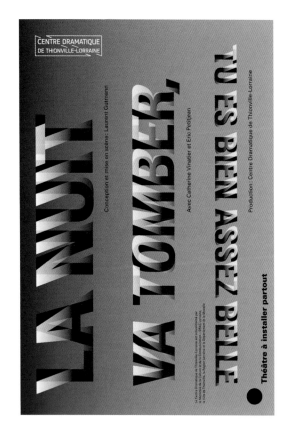

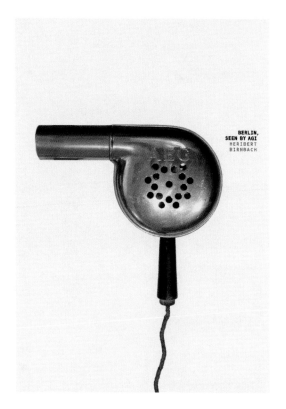

No. 0943

André Baldinger (b. 1963)
La nuit va tomber, tu es bien assez belle (theater poster), 2005
France

No. 0944

Heribert Birnbach (b. 1956)
Berlin, Seen by AGI, 2005
Germany

No. 0945

Michel Bouvet (b. 1955)
Photographie Arles, 2005
France

531

532

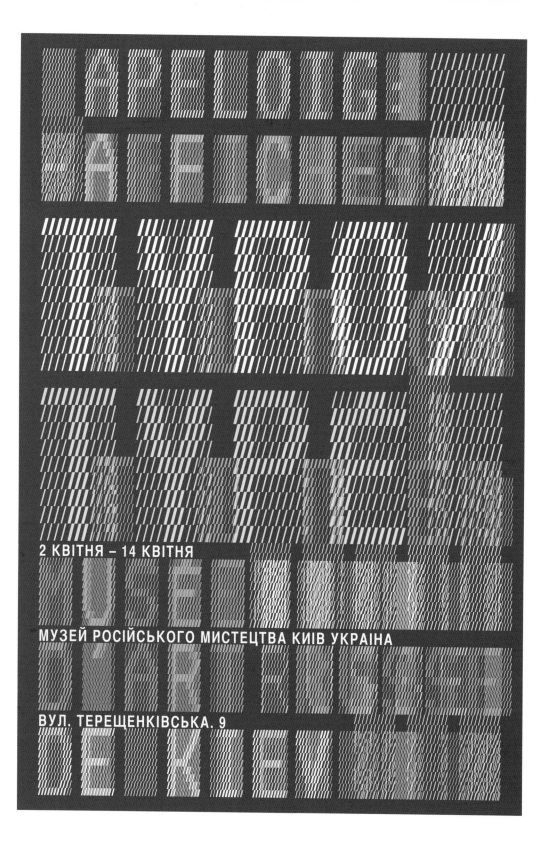

2 КВІТНЯ – 14 КВІТНЯ

МУЗЕЙ РОСІЙСЬКОГО МИСТЕЦТВА КИІВ УКРАІНА

ВУЛ. ТЕРЕЩЕНКІВСЬКА, 9

533

No. 0946

Philippe Apeloig (b. 1962)
Apeloig Affiches: Typo/Type
(exhibition poster), 2005
France

No. 0947

Leonardo Sonnoli (b. 1962)
AA (anno accademico,
poster for the University of
Venice), 2005
Italy

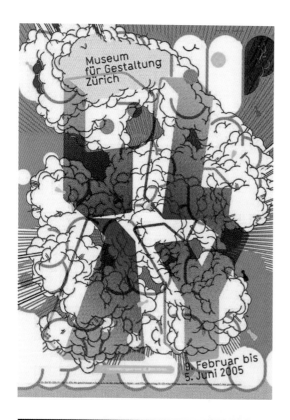

534

No. 0948
Martin Woodtli (b. 1971)
Play (exhibition poster),
2005
Switzerland

No. 0949
Lanny Sommese
Help (poster for the
Hurricane Poster Project),
c. 2004-5

No. 0950
Jian Zhao
Find Out Yourself, 2005
China

No. 0951
Leonardo Sonnoli (b. 1962)
*Berlin Seen by Leonardo
Sonnoli* (poster for an AGI
Congress), 2005
Italy

BERLIN-
SEEN BY

LEONARDO SONNOLI-CODESIGN

AGI CONGRESS 2005
IN BERLIN

photo by
massimo gardone-azimut
printed by
stella arti grafiche
in trieste
produced by
codesign, july 2005

535

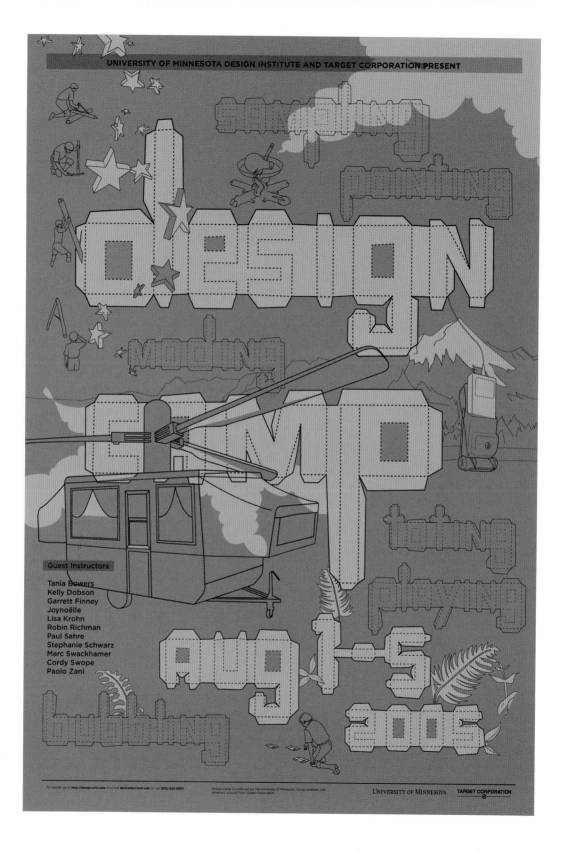

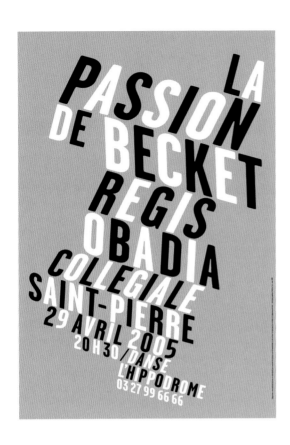

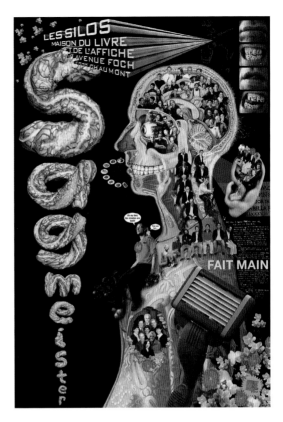

No. 0952
Paul Sahre
Design Camp, 2005
USA

No. 0953
Catherine Zask (b. 1961)
La Passion de Becket,
(poster for a dance
performance), 2005
France

No. 0954
Stefan Sagmeister (b. 1962)
Sagmeister: Fait Main
(exhibition poster),
c. 2004
France

No. 0955
Lex Reitsma (b. 1958)
L'amour des trois oranges
(opera poster), 2005
The Netherlands

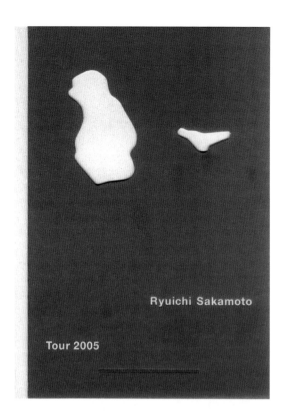

538

No. 0956
Hideki Nakajima
Ryuichi Sakamoto, 2005
Japan

No. 0957
Peter Moser
Du sollst nicht töten
(theater poster: *Hamlet*),
2005
Germany

No. 0958
István Orosz (b. 1951)
Berlin, 2005
Hungary

No. 0959
István Orosz (b. 1951)
Attila (tribute to Hungarian
poet Attila József), 2005
Hungary

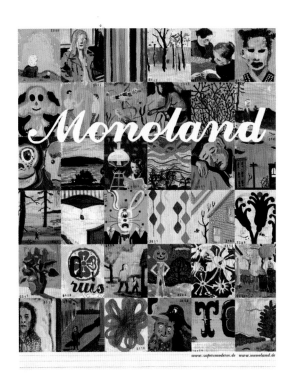

No. 0960 / No. 0961
Tommy Li (b. 1960)
Heromoism, 2005
Hong Kong

No. 0962
Atak (Georg Barber)
(b. 1967)
Monoland (poster for a rock
band), 2006
Germany

No. 0963
Ralph Schraivogel (b. 1960)
Schaffhausen Jazzfestival,
2002
Switzerland

No. 0964
Reza Abedini (b. 1967)
*Reza Abedini Poster
Exhibition*, 2006
Iran

No. 0965
Reza Abedini (b. 1967)
Iranian Imagination
(exhibition poster), 2006
Iran

No. 0966
Reza Abedini (b. 1967)
AllOne (exhibition poster),
2006
Iran

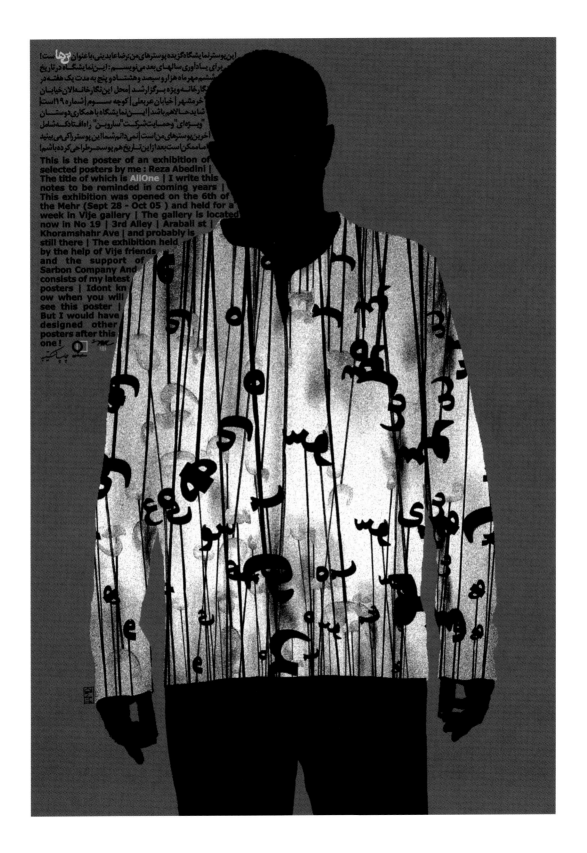

این پوسترنمایشگاه گزیده پوسترهای من نرضا عابدینی،با عنوان نرها است |
برای یادآوری سالهای بعد می نویسم : این نمایشگاه در تاریخ
ششم مهر ماه هزار و سیصد و هشتاد و پنج به مدت یک هفته در
نگارخانه ویژه بـرگزار شـد | محل این نگارخانه الان خیابان
خرمشهر | خیابان عربعلی | کوچه سـوم | شماره ۱۹ است |
شاید حالا هم باشد | این نمایشگاه با همکاری دوستان
"ویـژه ای" وحمایت شرکت "ساروین" راه افتاد که مشغل
آخرین پوسترهای من است | نمی دانم شما این پوستر را کی می بینید
اما ممکن است بعد از این تـاریخ هم پوستر طراحی کرده باشم!

This is the poster of an exhibition of
selected posters by me : Reza Abedini |
The title of which is AllOne | I write this
notes to be reminded in coming years |
This exhibition was opened on the 6th of
the Mehr (Sept 28 - Oct 05) and held for a
week in Vije gallery | The gallery is located
now in No 19 | 3rd Alley | Arabali st |
Khoramshahr Ave | and probably is
still there | The exhibition held
by the help of Vije friends
and the support of
Sarbon Company And
consists of my latest
posters | Idont kn
ow when you will
see this poster |
But I would have
designed other
posters after this
one !

543

546

fachverlag · professor-neu-allee 6 · 53225 bonn

proiecta

No. 0971
Bob van Dijk (b. 1967) and
NLXL
AGI, 2007
The Hague

No. 0972
Heribert Birnbach
Proiecta (promotional
poster for a publisher),
2007
Germany

No. 0973
Ben Faydherbe (b. 1958)
[Un]Building, 2007
(exhibition poster), 2007
The Netherlands

No. 0974
Ebrahim Haghighi
(b. 1949)
Seeking the Truth (poster
for a film festival), 2007
Iran

25th
Fajr
International
Film Festival
Tehran, Feb. 1-11, 2007

Seeking the Truth
Competition of Spiritual Cinema

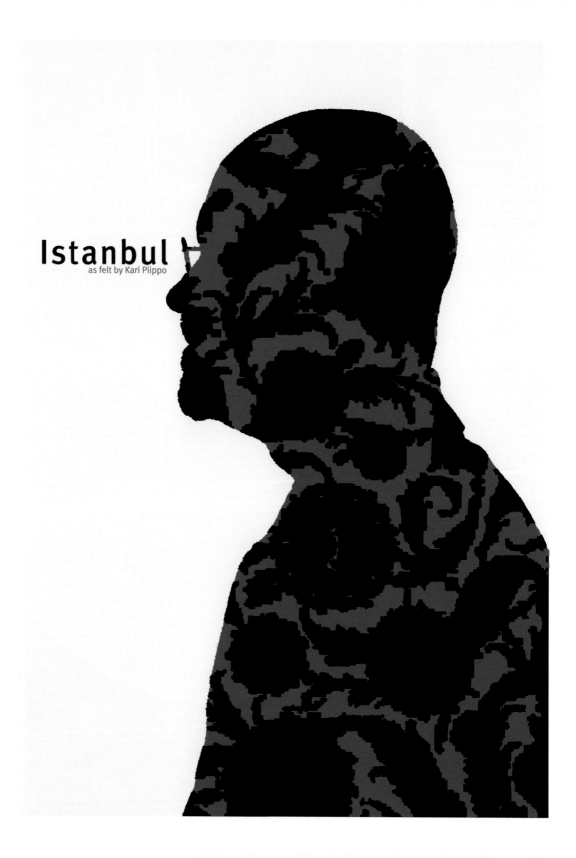

Istanbul
as felt by Kari Piippo

548

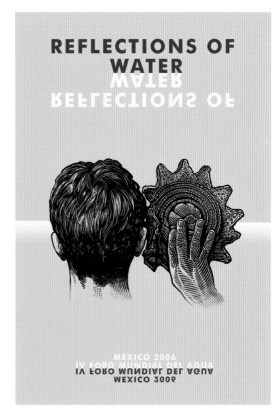

549

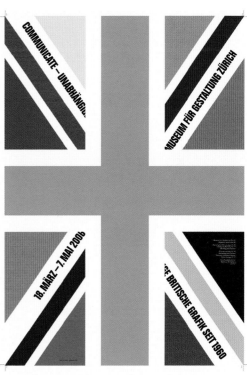

No. 0975
Kari Piippo (b. 1945)
Istanbul as felt by Kari Piippo, 2006
Finland

No. 0976
Ebrahim Haghighi
(b. 1949)
Eye of the Reality (poster for a film festival), 2006
Iran

No. 0977
István Orosz (b. 1951)
Reflections of Water (poster for a conference on water), 2006

No. 0978
Ralph Schraivogel (b. 1960)
Communicate—Independent British Graphic Design since 1960 (exhibition poster), 2006
Switzerland

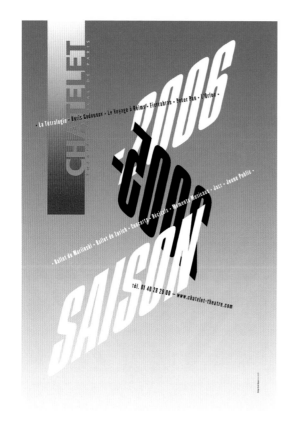

No. 0979
Rudi Meyer
Chatelet Saison 2005-2006
(theater poster), 2004
France

No. 0980
Lanny Sommese
Central Pennsylvania
Festival of the Arts, 2006
USA

No. 0981
Saed Meshki (b. 1964)
A Little Kiss (movie poster),
2005
Iran

یک بوس کوچولو

فیلمی از بهمن فرمان‌آرا

بازیگران: رضا کیانیان، جمشید مشایخی، هدیه تهرانی، جمشید هاشم‌پور، فاطمه معتمدآریا

طراح صحنه: فرهاد فارسی. موسیقی: احمد پژمان. تدوین: عباس گنجوی. مدیر فیلمبرداری: محمود کلاری

تهیه‌کننده: علیرضا شجاع‌نوری. نویسنده و کارگردان: بهمن فرمان‌آرا

552

ZEITBILDER
DNA Die Neue Aktionsgalerie
MELK IMBODEN Auguststrasse 20, Berlin
8. bis 17. September 2005
Öffnungszeiten der DNA Galerie: Dienstag – Freitag 14 – 19 Uhr, Samstag 11 – 19 Uhr und nach Vereinbarung

Art Center
DESIGNERPORTRAITS
Friedrichstrasse 134, Etage 6, Berlin, 16. bis 25. September 2005
Öffnungszeiten des Art Centers: Dienstag – Samstag 14 – 19 Uhr

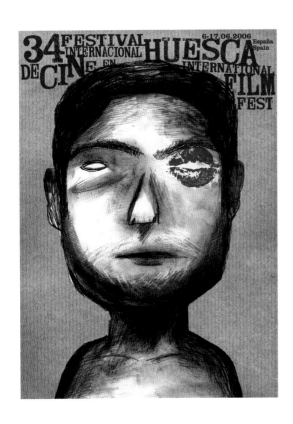

No. 0982
Melchior Imboden (b. 1956)
Zeitbilder: Melk Imboden
(exhibition poster), 2005
Germany

No. 0983
Alejandro Magallanes
(b. 1971)
*34th Huesca International
Film Festival*, 2006
Mexico

No. 0984
Dieter Feseke (b. 1957)
*8. Internationales Festival
für Stummfilm* (silent film
festival), 2006
Berlin

No. 0985
Keisuke Nagatomo
(b. 1939)
Asyura ni Gozansu (theater
poster), 1978
Japan

554

No. 0986
Paul Davis (b. 1962)
Pioneer, 2006
UK

No. 0987
Paul Davis (b. 1962)
*I Can Arrange Your
Mortgage For You*, 2006
UK

No. 0988
Paul Davis (b. 1962)
*You Are Not Alone: We Hate
Your Latest Work Too*, 2006
UK

YOU ARE NOT ALONE: WE HATE YOUR LATEST WORK TOO

556

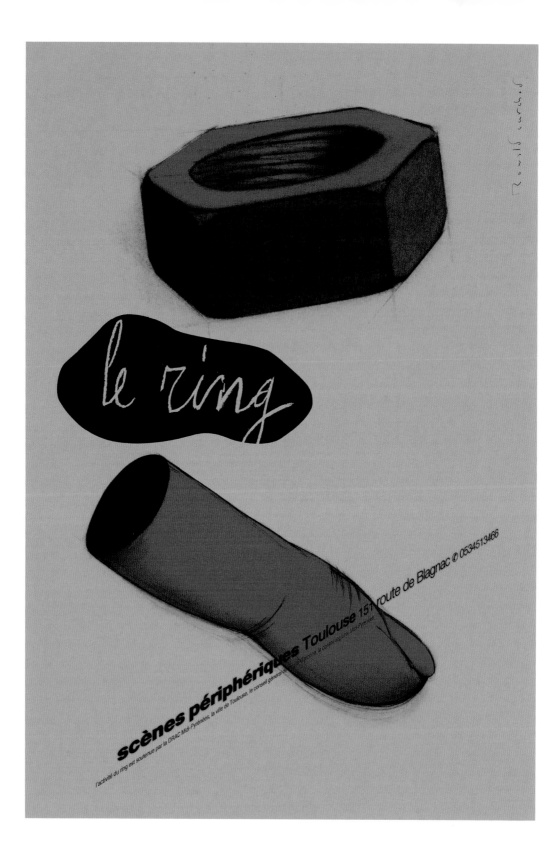

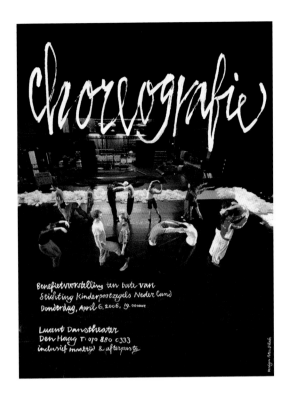

No. 0989

Ronald Curchod (b. 1954)
Le ring (poster for a theater
event), 2005-6
France

No. 0990

Stephan Bundi (b. 1950)
Mein Leben als Versager
(book poster: *My Life as a
Failure*), c. 1996
Cosmos Verlag, Muri-Bern,
Switzerland

No. 0991

Peter Bilak (b. 1973)
Choreografie (poster for a
dance workshop), 2006
The Netherlands

No. 0992

Philippe Apeloig (b. 1962)
Bateaux sur l'eau
(exhibition poster), 2003
France

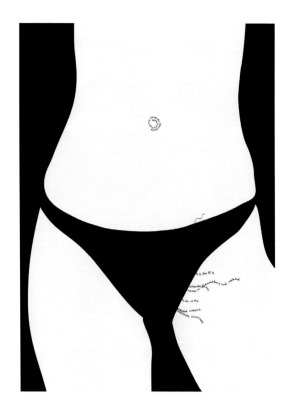

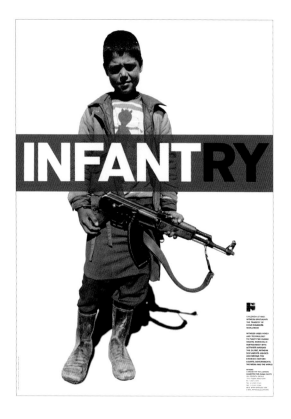

560

No. 0997
Fons Hickmann (b. 1966)
Clothing Collection (poster
for a conference center on
social and cultural issues),
2002
Germany

No. 0998
Harry Pearce (b. 1960)
Infantry (poster for
Witness, an international
human rights organization),
2007
USA

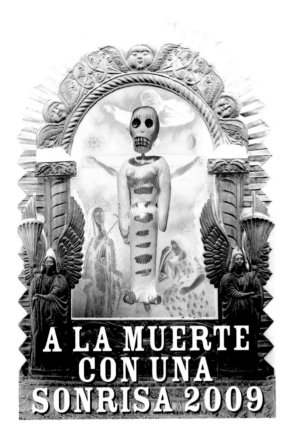

Act Live – Hong Kong International Poster Triennial 2010

No. 0999
Richard B. Doubleday
(b. 1962)
*A la muerte con una
sonrisa* (poster for a poster
competition in Mexico
City), 2009
Mexico

No. 1000
Richard B. Doubleday
(b. 1962)
*Act Live-Hong Kong
International Poster
Triennal 2010*, 2010
Hong Kong

562

INDEX

A

Aartomaa, Tapani, Nos. 0753, 0779, 0881
Abedini, Reza, Nos. 0932, 0964, 0965, 0966
Agullo, No. 0291
Allner, Walter Heinz, No. 0404
Andersen, Ib, No. 0338
Anton, Ottomar, No. 0176
Apeloig, Philippe, Nos. 0762, 0834, 0946, 0992, 0995, 0996
Armond, Mario, No. 0550
Arvanitis, Dimitris, Nos. 0794, 0938
Atak (Georg Barber), No. 0962
Atelier Ade, No. 0607
Atelier Hofmann, No. 0439
Atelier Lumax, No. 0234
Atelier Populaire, Nos. 0618, 0619, 0655
Avedon, Richard, No. 0616
Axelbuham Gruppe, No. 0651

B

Baaring, Maggi, No. 0366
Bade, Ingrid Louisa, No. 0269
Bailey, Bill, Nos. 0375, 0376
Bakst, Leon, No. 0114
Baldinger, André, Nos. 0796, 0797, 0878, 0943, 0993
Barber, Georg, Nos. 0812, 0826
Bass, Saul, Nos. 0494, 0495, 0501
Baumberger, Otto, Nos. 0156, 0188, 0255, 0383
Bayer, Herbert, Nos. 0161, 0419, 0615
Beardsley, Aubrey Vincent, No. 0011
Beckman, Anders, Nos. 0242, 0370, 0409
Beckman, Per, Nos. 0242, 0370, 0409
Beeke, Anthon, No. 0790
Beggarstaff Brothers, Nos. 0017, 0020
Bellenger, Pièrre, Nos. 0272, 0273
Berann, Heinrich, No. 0543
Berlage, Hendrik Petrus, No. 0007
Bernard, Francis, Nos. 0192, 0239
Bernard, Sargent, L., No. 0416
Bernardus, Johannes, No. 0232
Bernhard, Lucian, Nos. 0076, 0080, 0090, 0091, 0105, 0127, 0288
Berrère, Adrien, Nos. 0084, 0118
Biais, Maurice, No. 0053
Bieling, Jac, No. 0166
Bilak, Peter, Nos. 0900, 0991
Bill, Max, No. 0244
Binder, Joseph, Nos. 0208, 0304, 0403
Bingler, Manfred, No. 0564
Birnbach, Heribert, Nos. 0944, 0972
Biro, Mihaly, No. 0111
Blank, Richard, No. 0432
Boccasile, Gino, No. 0307
Boehm, Adolf, No. 0046
Bögelund, Thor, No. 0286
Bohatsch, Walter, Nos. 0941, 0942

Bonnard, Pierre, Nos. 0008, 0505
Bons, Jan, No. 0639
Boom, Irma, No. 0766
Bose, Günter Karl, Nos. 0829, 0880, 0899, 0901
Boucher, Pierre, No. 0444
Boullier, Robert, No. 0065
Bouvet, Michel, Nos. 0896, 0928, 0945
Boye, No. 0365
Brade, Helmut, Nos. 0813, 0828, 0927
Bradley, William H., Nos. 0019, 0022
Brandt, Peter (Artists and Writers Protest Group), No. 0671
Braques, Georges, No. 0493
Brasch, Sven, No. 0093
Breker, Walter, No. 0625
Brian de Kruyff van Dorsser, H. G., No. 0152
Brnadoly, J. S., No. 0148
Bromfield, Ken, No. 0437
Brun, Donald, Nos. 0352, 0379, 0472, 0492, 0504, 0537, 0624
Brusse, Wim, No. 0423
Brzozowski, Tadeusz, No. 0064
Bühler, Fritz, Nos. 0331, 0516
Bundi, Stephan, Nos. 0879, 0924, 0990
Burki, Charles, No. 0384
Burtin, Will, No. 0484
Büttner, Helmut Feliks, Nos. 0923, 0936
Butz, Fritz, No. 0385
Buzzi, Daniele, No. 0453
Byrd, Edward David, No. 0715

C

Calame, Georges, Nos. 0478, 0783
Calder, Alexander, No. 0542
Camps, Gaspar, No. 0163
Camy, H., No. 0397
Cao, Fang, Nos. 0849, 0892
Cappiello, Leonetto, Nos. 0061, 0067, 0097
Carabott, F. V., No. 0558
Carati, No. 0246
Carboni, Erberto, Nos. 0353, 0410, 0480
Cardinaux, Emile, No. 0079
Carigiet, Alois, Nos. 0292, 0326
Carlu, Jean George Leon, Nos. 0169, 0203, 0204, 0206, 0264, 0312, 0330, 0458
Caspel, Johann Georg van, No. 0045
Cassandre, A. M., Nos. 0165, 0185, 0186, 0193, 0215, 0262
Cassiers, Henri, Nos. 0014, 0050
Castiglioni, Luigi, No. 0601
Chastonay, P. H., No. 0500
Chéret, Jules, Nos. 0009, 0021, 0030, 0031, 0056
Chwast, Seymour, Nos. 0690, 0709
Cieslewicz, Roman, Nos. 0517, 0538, 0539, 0572, 0581, 0584, 0589, 0646

Clare, Etienne, No. 0271
Colin, Paul, Nos. 0195, 0205, 0289
Coppola, Silvio, No. 0691
Cretem, Victor, No. 0116
Croce, No. 0394
Crouwel, Wim, Nos. 0647, 0658, 0737
Curchod, Ronald, Nos. 0850, 0940, 0989
Cyan, Nos. 0771, 0772, 0808, 0809, 0863, 0890, 0920, 0922

D

d'Ache, Caran, No. 0018
Dalí, Salvador, No. 0662
David, Jean, No. 0512
Davis, Paul, Nos. 0986, 0987, 0988
Dawn Patrol, No. 0763
de Alvis, Michel, No. 0388
Dea Trier Morch (Denmark), No. 0670
de Faria, Candido Aragonese, No. 0069
de Feure, Georges, No. 0043
de Koo, Nicolaas Petrus, No. 0164
Delauney, Charles, No. 0360
Desmeure, Victor J., No. 0256
Deutsch, Ernst, No. 0119
de Vringer, Wout, Nos. 0837, 0905
Diggelmann, Alex W., No. 0364
Dollian, Guy, No. 0110
Domerque, Jean Gabriel, No. 0510
Dorzopykob, No. 0679
Doubleday, Richard B., Nos. 0999, 1000
Doyle, Stephen, No. 0864
Dradi, Carlo, No. 0461
Dransy, Jules Isnard, No. 0158
Droit, Jean, No. 0228
Dudovich, Marcello, Nos. 0060, 0086

E

Ebina, Tatsuo, Nos. 0851, 0877
Eckersley, Tom, No. 0703
Edel, Edmund, Nos. 0039, 0049
Edelmann, Heinz, Nos. 0741, 0748
Effel, Jean, No. 0656
Eidenbenz, Hermann, No. 0490
Elfer, Arpad, No. 0459
Elffers, Dick, No. 0524
Elzingre, Edouard, No. 0223
Emmerich, Maria Weninger, No. 0267
Engelhardt, Julius Ussy, No. 0180
Engelmann, Pavel Michael, Nos. 0431, 0434
English, Michael, Nos. 0600, 0636, 0637, 0638
Erdt, Hans Rudi, Nos. 0074, 0092
Erkelens, Paul, No. 0339
Erni, Hans, Nos. 0417, 0529
Escher, Gielijn, Nos. 0682, 0698
Excoffon, Roger, No. 0657
Exinger, Otto, No. 0319

567

Designer: Cees W. de Jong

Front cover: Stefan Sagmeister. *Set the Twilight Reeling, Lou Reed* (poster for CD), 1996

Back cover: Henri de Toulouse-Lautrec. *Ambassadeurs* (poster for a cabaret act), 1892

Library of Congress Cataloging-in-Publication Data:

Jong, Cees de.
   The poster : 1,000 posters from Toulouse-Lautrec
to Sagmeister / Cees W. de Jong,
Alston W. Purvis, Martijn F. Le Coultre.
     p. cm.
   Includes bibliographical references and index.
   ISBN 978–0–8109–9588–8 (alk. paper)
1. Posters—History. I. Purvis, Alston W., 1943- II.
Le Coultre, Martijn
F. III. Title. IV. Title: 1,000 posters from Toulouse-
Lautrec to Sagmeister.
V. Title: One thousand posters from Toulouse-Lautrec
to Sagmeister.
   NC1810.J66 2010
   741.6'7409—dc22
   2010014458

Printed and bound in Slovenia
10 9 8 7 6 5 4 3 2 1

Abrams books are available at special discounts when
purchased in quantity for premiums and promotions as
well as fundraising or educational use. Special editions
can also be created to specification. For details, contact
specialmarkets@abramsbooks.com or the address below.

ABRAMS
THE ART OF BOOKS SINCE 1949

115 West 18th Street
New York, NY 10011
www.abramsbooks.com